Options Trading
Simplified

Beginner's Guide to Make Money Trading Options in 7 Days or Less!

Learn the Fundamentals and Profitable Strategies of Options Trading

Table of contents

Chapter 1 – Getting Started in Trading Options

An old Chinese proverb says that every journey starts with a single step. And here you are starting out on day 1 of your quest to learn all about trading options and making money in 7 days or less! Options are complex there is no getting around that and there is a lot to learn in such a short time and it's difficult to know where to start. But as this book is aimed at the beginner – someone new to options and financial trading then starting with the basics is as good a place as any. So today on day 1, we will introduce you to the basic concepts and theory of Options, what they are, how they work for us and why we trade them.

By taking this journey one step at a time we will build your knowledge, chapter by chapter, with each subsequent chapter building on the concepts learned previously. By approaching the journey one step at a time you will learn and become comfortable with some of the complex theory, concepts and principles of options trading but importantly also learn the practical skills you will need to thrive in the Options market.

In This Chapter

You will learn:

- About why people are trading Options
- What are options?
- How did options come about?
- Comparing Options to other Financial Instruments

- Learn some of the key definitions
- Learn how options operate in theory and in practice
- How options are ultimately valued

Introducing Options

In financial trading, an option is a contract between two parties that gives one party – the prospective buyer - the choice between committing to a trade on a specific asset at an agreed price and at an agreed date and alternatively backing out of the trade. Therefore we can consider an Option to be a financial instrument that allows you the buyer to speculate on the market with low or at least identified risk. For example, as a beginner you may wish to test the water and so buy a stock option – this is a contract based on the underlying shares of a company - with a view to buying the underlying stock at a set price at a later predetermined date. The beauty of the Option is that should your assessment of the market be correct you can exercise your right to buy the shares or take your profit.

However, should your assessment be wrong and you have misjudged the market trend then you can simply walk away with no obligation to buy the stock. For example, a call option would let you select an Option today that is set at a fixed price which will be available to you at a future date. This means that you can assess the current price of the stock and then choose an option with an attractive future price, which you feel will maximize your profits. But, importantly, you are under no future obligation to buy the underlying stock – you can walk away for any reason.

Options Trading Simplified

Options are certainly not just tools for learning trading as institutional traders will use them regularly for what is known as Hedging where they buy options – importantly not the underlying stock - as insurance against a turn in their market position. This gives Options several unique characteristics which makes them valuable tools for insurance against risk.

Moreover, trading in Options is not just about hedging and insuring against risk it is also a very powerful way to make money if you know what you are doing. Unfortunately many rush in without fully grasping the technical details of Options and subsequently make large losses. This is simply because options are at first complex to grasp and even though they may well be based upon stocks and shares the mechanics of trading is very different.

This common perception of complexity and higher risk makes a lot of beginners and intermediary traders avoid trading in options. But it doesn't have to be that way because trading options is actually a good place for beginners and intermediary traders to start out because if done correctly it can limit losses and risk while at the same time increasing the potential for profits. However, we must not underestimate the difference in the levels of knowledge and skills that are required to successfully trade in options.

What Are Options?

An option is defined as a contract between two parties, which gives the holder (buyer) the right, but not the obligation, to buy or sell the underlying asset at an agreed fixed price at an agreed time in the future – or in some cases at any time before the contract's expiry date.

Options as we saw earlier were designed to allow institutional investors to mitigate risk and act as tools for ensuring against market unpredictability. Thus the Options contract was originally used to buy insurance against potentially catastrophic price movements that would have led to huge losses. But their inherent characteristics soon made Options attractive to traders as speculation tools in their own right. To see how Option became fashionable with traders we need to take a deeper dive into what makes up an Option contract.

An option is a contract based upon an underlying asset, a derivative, which means that an Option's value is derived from the underlying asset. In financial trading the underlying asset is usually stocks or a commodity, but it also can be the value of a market index or interest rate. Indeed in contract law it can be practically anything.

Options in Common Law

Options can be best explained and easiest understood using examples from everyday contract law as Option contracts have been in place since trade began. For example, suppose you want to buy a house or a new car, but you don't have a mortgage or finance at hand. In this case you would perhaps agree with a price with the seller and a date for completion of the sale. However the seller is going to want a deposit in return for this sales contingency, which gives you the right to buy at the agreed price at a future date or walk away from the sale if you change your mind. The deposit is compensation to the seller for providing you with the right, but not the obligation, to buy the car or house at the agreed price and date. If you renege on the deal and walk away, you will lose the deposit as that is the price of that option.

This is the basis of financial options, and if we consider the transaction through the lens of a financial trade we can substitute many of the technical terms to make the metaphor more transparent. So for example when you go to buy a house you agree to a price (strike price) and a date (expiry date) and a suitable deposit (premium) as part of the sales contingency (the Option contract). Then on the expiry date you will exercise your right to buy the house (stock) at the strike price or walk away (let the option expire) losing your deposit (premium).

Don't worry too much about some of the terms, such as strike price and premium all the trading jargon will be explained soon enough. What is important just now is that you understand that with Options trading you are dealing with a contract, the right to buy rather than the asset itself. But because that contract has inherent value, as it derives its value from the relationship between the strike prices, which is fixed in the contract, relative to the current market stock price. And if the contract is deemed attractive to others in the market then it also becomes a tradable asset in its own right.

Why Options Exist

An Option is considered in finance to be a derivative as it derives its value from an underlying asset. A stock option is similar to a contingency on the sale of a house or a deposit on a car but it involves the stock market rather than a private agreement.

For example, an Option - **MSFT 2019 Mar 39 call** - gives you the right to buy Microsoft at $39 per share at any time before the expiration date in mid-March 2019. If Microsoft is trading above $39 per share, you can exercise the option to buy and make a quick profit. The term, Exercising the option, is when you – the option holder - take up your contractual right to buy the shares at the agreed price – typically then to sell the stock on the market at the higher price for a tidy profit.

However, should the stock not perform as expected over the lifetime of the Option contract and the stock is selling below $39, then you would just let the contract expire as it makes no sense to buy a stock at a higher price than market value as you could buy the stock cheaper in the open market.

When an Option contract expires it means the value of the option is worthless and thus the loss to the buyer is 100% of the cost of the Option – the (deposit) Premium.

To get a better understanding of why they came about it is best to look at how they are used by taking a closer look at their use in practice.

Options as Insurance

As we touched on earlier Institutional and fund managers use stock options as a form of insurance. They want to protect themselves against any market turn-around and potentially damaging losses by having in-place a hedge bet, which is a counter-balance position. In effect they will be placing a bet that works in the opposite direction to the desired position of the asset they wish to protect thereby nullifying any adverse market movements. This works because with Options they are guaranteed a method to buy or sell stock at a specific price, but with no obligation to buy, before or upon a certain date.

So, for example, should they wish to protect the value of a portfolio, of let's say, their very expensive Amazon shares (that they own). Then they could do so by buying a relatively cheap Option that worked in favour of falling Amazon stock prices – i.e. its value increases as Amazon prices fall. In this way, even though their prized Amazon portfolio dropped in price their Option would be increasing in value and vice versa so together they would counter-balance any price fluctuations in the market.

This form of Hedging is often performed in order to protect against risk to a position or an asset. Institutional stock traders have always had in place complex and often costly methods of risk management. However, it was only in 1973 when there was the standardization of stock options that it finally made risk actually manageable and very cost effective.

Using options in this way allows institutional investors to ensure against price changes and is known as hedging. Institutional traders are willing to pay the price, known as a premium, to obtain this insurance.

Trading Options Basics

Learning Options trading is not trivial but it can be very rewarding if you learn the basic principles well and stick to good trading practices. The most important thing to learn as a beginner, as with all forms of financial trading, is the necessity of protecting your capital. The most profound way of doing this is by only paper trading – or using a test simulator – when you first start out. It is vital that you test your strategies and trading tactics with virtual money before you ever trade with real money.

Options trading, though is still deemed to be complicated and very risky, it is actually a good place for beginners to start out financial trading as it provides several safety nets. For example, in Options trading, a beginner, if they follow the correct strategies, will find that their risk and losses are limited but their potential profits are unlimited. This is simply down to the nature of Options in so much as you as a beginner will be trading in contracts called premiums rather than buying the underlying stock. Hence the extent of your losses is limited to the price of the premium – don't worry we will explain all this in detail later – for now it is enough to know that when trading options we can show you how to limit losses and risk while chasing unrestricted profits.

As this book is targeted at beginners it would be helpful first to give you a high-level summary as to why trading in options is advantageous. And the best place to start is to explain the mechanisms behind Option trading and how they work.

What is Options Trading?

When you trade in options you are trading in a contract based upon an underlying asset – typically a stock in a company. An Option is a contract that gives the holders the right but not the obligation, to buy or sell an asset in the future at a price determined today.

That definition is hugely important to understand as it is the basic concept of Options Trading – basically you are buying the right to buy the underlying shares but are under no obligation to do so. So should the price go against your position you can simply walk away albeit you will lose the cost of the option but no more. Hence, despite the common belief of it being a high-risk pursuit, trading in Options is much less risky than buying stocks outright where losses and profits are unlimited.

However there is another attractive characteristic of trading in Options and that is due to the fact that you can as a beginner trade safely in high-value stocks that would generally be out with your budget. This is because when you buy an Option you are not actually buying the stock but the future right to buy at a fixed price. Therefore, the option is priced at only a fraction of the actual stock price.

This means that you can buy an option in high volume, volatile stock such as Apple, Amazon, etc., which would give you the control over 100 shares for perhaps $100, whereas to buy 100 shares of these premier stocks would set you back thousands of dollars. Remember, as there is no obligation to buy the shares you can simply take your profit and walk away – no questions asked.

Indeed as there is no obligation to exercise the Option itself it also becomes a tradable asset – and this is what came about. Instead of traders exercising their rights to buy the underlying asset many simply bought the Options to trade on the open market. However for every deal there must be a buyer and a seller – so other traders soon began writing Options in order to fulfil the market demand. Hence the flourishing market in Options we see today.

Options are extremely flexible so are used as both a form of insurance and as a source of speculative profits. The value is largely derived from the value of an underlying asset or financial instrument, but it also has additional components such as time till expiration, and a locked-in price that provides additional value. So the value of the Option is not solely determined by the current value of the underlying asset or security as there are several other factors that come into play.

Moreover Options provide the beginner the right level of entry into the market if they have only limited funds and trading knowledge. Furthermore, the beginner can despite their lack of experience and trading skills also trade well above their budget and leverage their account to trade diligently in a low risk and high reward strategy. But Options are not just attractive to beginners with limited funds for in financial trading Options provide ways for experienced traders to add options on individual stocks, indexes, and exchange-traded mutual funds (ETFs) to their investment portfolio.

Nonetheless, the best reason for a beginner to start trading in Options and an intermediary level trader to add options to their trading or investing strategies is that Option trading allows you to both manage risk while at the same time allowing you to optimize profits. And because there are so many different methods and techniques to trade in options there is a wide market for both buyers and sellers – i.e. just about anyone can benefit from trading them, so let look at some traditional examples.

If we contemplate the traditional buy and hold strategy for stocks, which is a good example, as that is the way that long term investors operate. In this scenario we can consider it to be akin to you owning (real estate) apartments and then taking income as rent through properties per month for long periods to generate year-on-year income.

Now this is a good way to generate long term safe income. However this patient strategy may not work so well when you want short term profits and large gains. In which case, the way to generate quick returns would be to rent out your apartment short term at higher rates via Airbnb. In which case, a financial trading metaphor would be to shift away from trading in stocks and mutual funds to invest in writing (selling) short term Options based upon your stock portfolio.

Comparing Options to other Securities

Options are a form of financial derivative, and all that means is that it derives its value from an underlying security. For example, a common type of Option is the Stock options - which this book focuses on – and they derive their value from the underlying company stock's market performance. However Options can and are traded using other derivatives such as commodities and exchange-traded mutual funds (ETF):

- **Commodities and futures**

    The provenance of financial Options are in the trading of Commodity and Futures contracts as these were agreements between two parties typically farmers and traders looking for a future price for their next harvest crops. The futures markets developed to help traders hedge and speculate on commodities, especially in the agricultural market. The options market in turn evolved from the futures market, hence, the similarities and the shared concepts. But, because commodities and futures deal with a physical asset there are slight differences as to how they work. The seller of a commodity or futures option is still obligated to buy or sell stock. However, exercising the contract is different as commodities and futures contracts set the price for delivery of a specific quantity of a physical item – a bushel of wheat, for example - to be delivered to a particular location on an agreed date. There is nothing similar in stock options as there is no need for a physical delivery of anything. Commodity options are options listed on such things as corn, oil, gold, or interest rates.Futures on the other hand are options trading on the underlying value of futures contracts, typical futures on commodities and currencies. Futures contracts are therefore derivative contracts – their value is derived from the underlying commodity/asset - that give holders the obligation to buy or sell an asset at a specified future date for a specified price. Where there is a similarity between stock options and commodities and futures contracts is that they lock in the price and quantity of an asset and have predetermined expiration dates. But in both cases, they are in themselves tradable assets, which means you can trade away your rights and obligations if you wish to exit the contract early.

- **Equity options**

An equity option is an option based on the price of a share of stock of a company. However options are not available on all stocks but some do not have options attached to them. It is up to the exchanges to determine whether or not to offer an option – based upon perceived demand – it is not up to the companies that issue the stock.

Most equity options are priced at 1 contract per 100 shares. Equity options are what most people think of when they contemplate Options.

- **Index Options**

The concept behind trading options in indexes is that if you can buy an option on a stock of a particular company within a sector say technology then why does the exchange not make available an option on that market sector as a whole? That's the idea behind index options you can bet on the sector performance and not have to drill down to a specific company.

The result has been a proliferation of Index options based on the performance of different market indices. There are options on the S&P 500, NASDAQ, and FTSE. Trading in indexes has become a very popular alternative to trading in stock options as they can represent a collection of diverse assets. This means that a trader can spread their investments across several sectors of interest. The index worksby pooling together several stocks in the same sector or across diverse sectors and the performance aggregate is used to measure the price of the group. There are many indexes and these include stocks, commodities, and futures as they are all used as components of an index. But an index is just a logical category a convenient grouping of other securities so you can't buy an index directly. Instead, you buy a security thattracks the value of the index. An example of such an option would be one that tracked a particular ETF that owned the stocks in a particular index such as Standard & Poor's (S&P) 500Index.

- **Exchange traded funds (ETFs)**

ETFs are mutual funds that have become very popular trading vehicles as they can be traded like stocks on an exchange. Most ETFs are designed to track an index or an underlying sector so technically ETFs are not derivatives. However they are often referred to as quasi-derivatives. This is because unlike other indexes they can be traded and also because they are not necessarily holding exactly the same securities of the index that they are tracking. For example, some leveraged ETFs use swaps to mimic the action of the underlying index while adding leverage. ETFs allow you to trade on their underlying indexes, directly or through options. One of the most popular and well known ETFs is the S&P 500 SPDR (SPY).

- **Stocks and bonds**

Buying a company's stock gives you part ownership in that company, whereas buying bonds makes you a debt holder. Each position has its risks and rewards. However when we bring Options into the equation we can see that the three assets, stocks, bonds, and options, have very different risk and reward profiles.For example, although stocks give you a piece of the company, and bonds offer you income, options offer you no ownership of any tangible assets but all three can lead to a total loss of investment. In the end, stocks offer indefinite holding periods, and bonds have a maturity date, whereas options have a limited life based on their expiration date.

- **Interest Rate Options**

These are sometimes better known as *yield-based options,* as they trade on the interest rate on a specific type of bond. With this type of Option, calls (buying) become more valuable as interest rates rise, and interest rate puts (selling) become more valuable as the rates fall. Importantly, the underlying value is the interest rate and not the value of the bond itself. Because interest rates aren't securities and can't be traded or exchanged as such the settlement is in cash.

- **Miscellaneous Options**

The way that the different options exchanges make money and compete with one another is when they develop new innovative types of contracts that capture the imagination of hedgers and speculators. As an option is just a contract, which is based on the price of another asset options can be drawn up for just about anything where someone might want to guarantee a price and someone else might want to speculate on that price. As a result, exchanges are always trying out new option types so you can find options on different measures of market sentiment, *i.e.* whether it's optimistic or pessimistic about different economic outcomes.

- **A swap**

This is a type of insurance contract whose terms are privately agreed upon by the participants. It is an over-the-counter style option as they are non-exchange traded options. They are often used to bet on the direction of just about anything, including the weather, that the two parties agree upon. Swaps are by design sophisticated securities and so they are not available to individual investors. This is due to the lack of regulations and the often complex financial and legal requirements required to be signed before you can trade them.

Trading in Options

As opposed to investing in stock or assets, trading Options is often a decision based upon a short term analysis. An Option having a predetermined time period, a time-to-live, will have by design an expiry date. As a result Options are renewable and can be resold many times. This makes them suitable for both trading over the short term or over longer periods delivering income when the value of the underlying stock rises, falls, or even moves sideways.

Trading Options for Profit

Now the whole purpose of trading is that you want to have more money in the future than what you have just now. Therefore, to increase your wealth you are trading Options supplied by the markets. But here is the thing, regardless of the time frame — the question will come down to whether you have a tendency to hold a position for a short or long time — your objective after all will be the same too make more money.

Options Trading Simplified

But here is the problem because that hunger to make a profit makes traders and especially beginners impatient. Therefore as a beginner you should consider that every time that you contemplate a new trading strategy you will also have to contemplate a new learning curve. As a result, be prepared to realize that every change in strategy or trading tactics will begin with a deep study and analysis of trade conditions. This is where paper trading or virtual trading becomes invaluable as it lets you experiment with virtual cash and practice tactics with zero risks. Always be careful that when you start to trade with real cash that losses can be amplified so always be patient and be prepared to diligently spend the time required learning how to trade safely, or you will likely lose a lot of money on worthless premiums.

Regardless of the type of financial trading that you are undertaking there are some simple steps that you should adhere to in order to trade safely. It doesn't matter if you are a beginner or an intermediary trader it is always sensible to ensure that you protect your capital. This means that even if you are experienced in other forms of trading or investing, or even have experience with options but with different assets, you should always seriously contemplate the following:

- **Check your financial health**

  This means simply to check your financial balance sheet and your disposable income. This is hugely important as before you start trading in Options or any other financial instrument you must realize how much you can afford to lose. Therefore you must go over your finances diligently, and make sure that the amount that you have as trading capital is indeed disposable income. This means reviewing your current loans, mortgages, and life and health insurances as well as school fees or college funds.

- **Draw up a financial net worth statement**

  The purpose here is to ensure that you are aware of the amount you could lose and the desire to make profits – be sure you are comfortable with the risk/reward ratio. Also try and make sure that your finances are healthy and understand why you are taking on extraordinary risk.

- **Be realistic**

  Don't chase unrealistic goals and trade beyond your experience or safe capital levels. Furthermore, never risk more than 5% of your capital on any one trade – for beginners 1%-3% is the recommended maximum.

- **Know your own risk appetite**

  If you are a typically a cautious trader or a gambler, that may indicate that you may not be a good options trader. Nonetheless, there may be many trading option tactics and strategies that will suit your risk appetite. The thing to remember is that once you understand the built-in safety nets that trading options provides then it will decrease your risk. An important caveat is that just make sure you read through the book and stick to the beginners' strategies and tactics and find the ones that make you comfortable before you jump in.

- **Analyze the Data**

  Stocks trading places a lot of emphasis on technical analysis, fundamental analysis and Charts in order to maximize your chances of trading options successfully. Option trading rides upon the underlying stock so it also places a high emphasis on improving your technical and fundamental analysis skills. Therefore, you should be a diligent analyst, especially in identifying and following the dominant trends, as well as being able to analyze charts and the behavior of the underlying assets in your options.

- **Always test your strategies before putting them into practice**

  Testing out scenarios and tactics beforehand through paper trading before you take real-life risks is essential. Testing out theories before committing them with real money is always an excellent idea that is certain to provide both practices as well as saving you a lot of money

- **Never trade with money that you aren't willing to lose**

  This might seem strange as Options are often seen as being risk management tools. But even though options are often deemed to be risk-management vehicles, you can still lose money trading them – sometimes in the case of insurance that is the whole purpose. And if you should adopt more sophisticated and riskier option strategies; your potential losses should always be identified and

accepted as they could be significant if your trades –
especially- sell- if they are not thoroughly investigated
and analyzed beforehand.

Chapter 2 - Understanding Options

On the first day of our journey we learned about options, what they are and how they are used in financial trading both for hedging and for speculation. We also learned that Options are derivatives that derive their value from an underlying asset but they can act as financial instruments in their own right because they do have value. We also learned that an Options contract is based upon the value of another underlying asset or security such as a company's stock. Most commonly, the focus of trading options is mainly on those instruments with a value based on stocks and market indexes, although there is also a flourishing market and exchange for trading mutual funds (ETFs). In day 2, of your quest you will lift up the bonnet and take a look at what components and mechanisms make up an Option and see the different types that are available.

In This chapter you will learn:

- Under the bonnet – the components of an Option
- Options for Risk Management
- Option Contract Essentials
- Valuating Call Options
- Valuating Put Options
- Understanding Time and Time Decay
- Paper Trading
- Advantages of Option Trading

An Option's Components

There are only two basic types of options: calls (buying) and puts (selling). However, for the beginner considering entering the Options trading market they should initially restrict themselves to buying call options. This is purely a safety measure because if you stick to trading calls (buying) to start with and limit your position size you will not lose your trading fund. This is simply because when buying calls you are on the low-risk side of the deal as you own the rights. Trading puts (selling) places you on the other side of the trade with the obligations now on you and for a beginner that is no place to be.

Nonetheless as you learn more and become comfortable with the way Options work you can add the other types of options to your trading toolbox. The advantage of becoming competent in using both puts and calls is that it will add diversity to your investing and trading strategies. This is simply because you will now have the tools and the knowledge to participate in both bull (rising) and bear (falling) markets.

Furthermore, you can learn how to use options to limit your portfolio risk i.e. to protect an individual existing position such as a stock or ETF. It is also possible to develop a strategy to generate income through specific strategies known as spreads and writes however these are not for the beginner or the faint-hearted.

Know the underlying asset

Whatever way you decide to tactically trade in Options it is imperative that you fully understand the asset on which they're based. For example in this book the focus is on stock options and so this requires a deep understanding of how stocks trade and behave in the market. This will require that you have a thorough understanding and competency in technical and fundamental analysis and detailed chart analysis. For example, you will often be speculating against a strike price being exceeded during a fixed time period so you will need to have a deep understanding of the underlying stock's price movements. This cannot be down to just guesswork you must make these decisions based upon sound data analysis.

Another interesting element that needs to be studied is stock volatility as it is also a key component of options prices. With regards volatility you will have to look at the underlying stock's market volatility as part of your analysis in order to pick the best possible option for your particular strategy.

Risk Management

However even if you are buying options as insurance or as risk-management tools your primary focus is to understand the risks associated with the use of these tools, including all of the following:

- Knowing what conditions, both in the markets and in the individual security, to consider when analyzing a trade
- Using proper trade mechanics when creating a position
- Recognizing, understanding, and following trading rules and requirements for the security
- Understanding what individual variables make any position gain and lose value

It is therefore vital that you learn the key components of options trading so as to give you a sound foundation for designing rewarding strategies, tactics and positions that ensure that any losses are limited before they become catastrophic.

Option Contract Essentials

As we learned earlier a listed stock option, a standardized option that is traded on an exchange, is a contractual agreement between two anonymous parties. All listed options are standardized contracts, which are regulated and enforced using the same set of standard rules. Therefore, when you buy or sell an option i.e. you create a new trading position then you will be initiating one of two things, either:

- You are acquiring a specific set of rights, if you are buying or
- You are acquiring a specific set of obligations should you be selling.

It is imperative that as a beginner that you understand your rights and obligations, which are dependent on the position that you take by becoming either a buyer or a seller of an Option. These rights and obligations are standardized for options trading around the globe and are guaranteed by the national or regional authorities such as in the US the Options Clearing Corporation (OCC). Therefore you do not need to worry about the legality or the enforcement of the contract or even who you are making the agreement with as of course almost all trades will be anonymous.

Another important aspect of Options which you as a beginner need to understand is the role that time plays in the process.

Options Trading Simplified

Time is hugely important when trading in options as you are betting your position against a timeline.

Moreover, you are stating that your position will come good before or on a fixed expiry date. It's no good it coming good a day later it must come good sometime before or on that date. Therefore it is crucial that you plan your position with time being at the forefront of your thoughts. After all should Apple stock dive, it is no good thinking, ah, well Apple will definitely rise, so let's buy an option – you need to know when it will rise, will it be this week, next week, or in two months.

Understanding the Risk Components

This means that in trading Options the primary risks involved are compounded by two elements, 1) time sensitivity, which you don't need to be so aware of when trading in stocks and 2) leverage, this is the ability to generate disproportionate movement in option prices relative to your funds. Leveraging lower priced Options to control 100 stocks allows for larger percentage gains – and losses.

 Time is a very important factor when buying an Option as the price of a call option will increase the longer the available time span. This is intuitive as the longer the time period that the Options remains valid the higher the probability that your position will become valid and reach the strike price. This is simply because an Options value will go up or down depending on the underlying stock's movement. However the catch is in getting not just the price movement correct it's about getting it to coincide with the time span of the Option. This is critical because even if you speculate successfully the direction of the price movement of the underlying stock should the move in the stock come about too late then the Option will expire worthless.

Therefore when you are evaluating which option to buy or later when you become more experienced and start to write Options – you must expect to pay more – effectively buy yourself time – for Options that have longer expiration periods. Typically Options will range from a few weeks to 9 months or even up to 2 years to the expiration date and obviously the price will reflect the timespan.

Placing a Value on Call Options

Nonetheless, an Option's valuation is volatile for as we have seen Time Decay does play a major role – an Option loses value every day in the countdown to the expiration date – but it also fluctuates due to the performance of the underlying stock price relative to the strike price. This is because when you own Call Options, your rights allow you to;

- Buy a specific quantity typically 100 shares of the underlying stock (exercise your rights).
- Buy the 100 shares in the stock by a certain date (expiration date).
- Buy the specific quantity of stock at a specified price (strike price).

With those points in consideration we can see that the value and the price of the Call Option rises when the underlying stock price goes up because the price of the rights you bought through the option is fixed while the underlying stock itself is fluctuating in value – hopefully trending upwards in price.

Placing a Value on Put Options

On the other hand, should you hold a Put Option then it gains value when the underlying stock falls in price. When you hold a Put Contract you have the following rights:

- Sell a specific quantity typically 100 shares of the underlying stock (exercise your rights).
- Sell the 100 shares in the stock by a certain date (expiration date).
- Sell the specific quantity of stock at a specified price (strike price).

The right to sell a specific quantity (100) of stock by a certain date at a specified price is very beneficial in a bear market when prices are going downhill. For example if you hold a Put Option with a strike price of $60 you own the rights to sell that stock at $60. Now the thing to remember here is that the contract is between you and the Option writer – so they are in effect obliged to buy the stock from you the Option holder at the strike price in this case $60. The Option writer is hoping (betting) that the price stays above $60 but stock markets can be unpredictable and volatile so events such as bad news about the company's ability to match forecasted earning may push the stock price below $60m say to $50. Should that be the case, then you will find that the Put Option you are holding has become much more valuable. This is simply because the Put Option writer will be obliged to buy the underlying stock from you at $60 even though its current market value is significantly less.

In either case whether it be a Call or a Put Option the direction of the movement in price must occur before the option contract expires. If it fails to meet the strike price regardless of whether it is a Call or Put your option will expire and unfortunately be worthless.

Understanding Time and Time Decay

Therefore we cannot stress enough that success in trading Options will depend on your ability to select suitable options. The Options must have a target strike price as well as have an optimal timespan to the expiration date, which will allow sufficient time for the anticipated stock price movement to occur.

Not all stocks have options available for trading but many do have derived options. These listed options will be available in multiple expiration dates and strike prices. Indeed, as the trading of Options requires a buyer and a seller, you may find that making a bid on a strike price will trigger another trader to write an option to accommodate you. Hence, many Options are available but many are written to meet market demand. And this is another key element which we will contemplate later – you don't need to own the underlying stock in order to write an Option and many do not. These traders are speculating on the probability that the price fluctuation on the underlying stock will stay within certain boundaries – but that's certainly not for beginners. Nonetheless, before you jump in there are two caveats around Options pricing to keep in mind:

- Options with longer time periods until the expiration date will be more expensive
- Options with strike prices closer to the current underlying stock value are more expensive

You should now understand how trading in Options differs from trading in the underlying stocks. Options represent a contract that provides— leverage, rights or obligations, as well as a locked in price whereas stocks are an asset which represents partial ownership of a company. But there is another key difference as stocks in the market are limited in numbers, which creates their value but the number of options available is unlimited as they can be created on demand – remember you don't need to own stock to write an Option. Therefore, as you can see there are several important considerations that must be taken into account when trading Options as opposed to stocks. It is these distinctions that necessitate diligent trading and decision-making, which is beyond the basic buy or sell decisions based solely on price.

Moreover for the beginner it must be considered part of the learning process, when shifting from stock trading to options trading to develop a new but complementary way of approaching trading strategy and tactics. This new way of thinking will not just focus on the price of the underlying stock, but also on other factors, such time-decay, demand for the option and the overall market conditions – whether it is bullish or bearish. You will need to monitor your Option performance with time in mind and as the trade develops, you will need to have a strategy in mind as you may want to trade the option, exercise your rights to buy or sell and pocketing the profits or simply walk away taking any losses on the chin.

At present and as a beginner this may sound way too much information and way too difficult, but it will become much clearer as you read the next few chapters. Soon it will start to make sense as it all clicks into place because successful options trading is all about giving yourself and the Option time to deliver on your expectations.

Of course, Options trading is not all new as there are some basic trading tactics and best practices that carry over from other forms of trading, such as sound fund management techniques, entry and exit planning, as well as chart and technical analysis. Of the most profound example is in planning your exit for in Options trading there are several choices in exiting a position so it is not simple but it is an essential part of any trade. Therefore having clear objectives and an exit strategy will save you money in the long term should a position not develop as hoped or starts to move against you.

Paper Trading

If you haven't traded options or for that matter any other financial instrument in the past, they always try out your trading strategies on paper. It is always best to paper trade before you take the big step in using real money. Use live data and then see how your strategy works out. Paper trading isn't perfect as it can be boring – it lacks the psychological engagement of using real money – but it can uncover weaknesses in your strategy or tactics very quickly and cheaply. Your over-riding ambition when paper trading is to learn and try out different strategies, which as a beginner is essential practice.

Ultimately, you would want to be comfortable in your option trades as well as having a deep understanding of the underlying stock. So, before you contemplate trading using a live account and risking real money, you must have experience, skill and:

- An understanding of the recent market activity and characteristics of the underlying stock in the Options you are trading.
- Be comfortable recognizing market patterns and responding by mixing specialist strategies to match particular market scenarios.
- Be clear on your objectives per Option and have exit strategies in mind that will best deliver your goals.

As you can perhaps now begin to see that trading competently in the underlying asset of the Option, whether that is in stocks or indexes, is a prerequisite for successful Option trading. You can be expert in stocks or index trading and have never heard of options trading but the reverse is simply not true. To be a successful Options trader you must have deep knowledge of the underlying asset.

The Advantages of Option Trading

We could look at Option trading as being a supplemental skill to the other types of financial trading. But the additional work required to gain those skills will be worth it. To understand why let us reiterate the advantages of Options trading:

1. Better cost efficiency through leverage – a trader can gain a similar trading position as they could with stocks but with a much lower investment (cost of the stock vs. cost

of the Option premium). Similarly an Option controls 100 shares minimum so for the price of the premium you get to leverage the control and the benefits associated with 100 or more shares.

2. Lower risk – The risk in trading stock is linear and 1:1 both for-profit and loss. With Options losses are limited to the cost of the premium and no more, while potential profits remain limitless and linear (1:1)

3. Higher percentage returns – Options return huge percentage gains as opposed to direct stock trading as the cost of the trade – the premium - is miniscule in comparison to the actual stock price. The result is in most cases slightly lower dollar value as you have to subtract the cost of the premium but a much higher percentage return on investment.

4. Greater flexibility – Options allows a trader to speculate on a bull –upwards trend -, a bear – a downwards trend, and also a sideways (no-direction) moving trend. This provides for a wealth of investment alternatives which we will consider later in the book.

Considering these advantages alone and especially when you take into the equation the considerable value of risk reduction and potentially optimized profits it seems a no-brainer to trade in Options.

Chapter 3 – Putting Options to Work

On Day 2 of our journey we took a good look under the bonnet to see the components that make up a standard Put or Call Options. We saw how they comprised several elements that contributed to their valuation and how the underlying stock price, the strike price, expiry time, volatility and time-decay all play an important part in an Options Valuation. Then we learned the importance of safe trading through paper trading to test out our strategies and hone our skills and finally we recapped on the advantages of trading on Options over trading in the underlying stocks themselves.

Today in day 3 of the quest we will turn our attention to putting Options into practice in diverse market conditions and learn how Options can be deployed to take advantage of any movement in price whether that is up, down or sideways. We will learn just how flexible and useful Option strategies can be in profiting even in difficult market conditions.

In this Chapter

We will learn:

- How to deploy Put Options
- How to limit risk
- How to trade in a bear market
- How to trade in a difficult market
- How to make money in a flat market

- How to trade in EFTs
- Take a deeper dive in Option Calls and Puts
- About Option mechanisms
- About the pros and cons of Leverage

For the beginner to trading Options the transition from direct stock trading may appear to be complicated but the actual differences in trading stock and options are down to the obscure – at first – but actually pretty basic mechanics of placing the orders.

Ultimately, the advantages you will get from trading options will outweigh any disadvantages as they just provide you with a mechanism (leverage) to control the rights to the stock rather than the stock itself. This for the beginner is a big thing as it allows you to trade in options on expensive premier stocks, such as Amazon, Facebook and Apple. These stocks are very expensive but they also have big dollar moves. They are also typically out with the reach of beginners or traders of limited funds but with options they become accessible to the beginner for a fraction of the cost compared to buying and trading on the shares themselves.

Options Put to good use

Options are very flexible tools and can be deployed optimally in a number of diverse ways to maximize the risk-reward ratio. Options deployed in this manner will deliver the best mix of profit and risk reduction. A good example of this type of flexibility and out-of-the-box thinking is when an Option is deployed as insurance for an asset.

Hedging your Bets

The way the Options work as an insurance policy is what is called hedging and this is when you buy an option contract that works in the opposite direction to the asset being protected. The primary goal of a hedge is that the value of the option goes in the opposite direction of the underlying stock. This might be counter-intuitive but if we consider that you hold stock in Apple and so to protect the value of this holding and insure against any unlikely but catastrophic plunge in their value you would take out a Put Option. You would basically bet that the Apple stock will fall so that in effect should the Apple stock fall in value the Option will gain value and vice versa. The purpose of the Put Option would be to ensure that the total value of the combined position retains as much of the portfolio's value as is possible.

When using options as a way to manage risk you should be aware:

- You can manage risk for an existing position either fully or partially. With the latter you will need to monitor and adjust the hedging process based upon the market changes.
- You can also consider managing risk for a new position at a low price using a single long-term option or through deploying a combination of options.

This is typically a good use for a PUT Option and demonstrates another reason as to why there are always buyers and sellers in the Options market. After all not everyone is in trading Options for the same reasons and there will always be traders and investors as well as speculators, those looking for profit and those looking for insurance.

Trading in a Bear Market

The flexibility of Options trading is also apparent when speculating in a bear market – a downward trend with falling prices. This is because if you are bearish and are looking to capitalize from a falling market, options are a good tool for the purpose. Options will be much less expensive and have much lower risk exposure to dollar losses than the highly risky method of borrowing individual stock on a margin account to sell short.

Using Options in Challenging Markets

As we have seen Options have the flexibility to allow you to trade in bull and bear markets. Options are the perfect tool in many ways for trading in those rising or falling markets through stocks or other underlying instruments. Now that is not to say that you couldn't do the same indirect stock trading, assuming of course that you are comfortable with both owning or borrowing these securities and selling them short.

However where Options have a distinct – but risky- advantage is in the case of a sideways market, where a stock is doing nothing just fluctuating around the same price week after week and with little trade volume. With direct stock trading there isn't a lot you can do but with Options you could craft strategies for sideways markets whether you possess any underlying stock or not. These are high-risk strategies which are not suitable for beginners but we will cover them nonetheless later in the book. But for now we will just present a high-level introduction.

Making Money in Flat Markets

When you hear the term Directional bias in financial trading it refers to the link between profits and the overall direction of prices. For example, in traditional trading in order to profit when you are long – holding or buying the stock- you need prices to go up. Conversely, to profit when you're short – selling or borrowing stock - you need prices to fall. However what can be done when prices are flat and stagnating?

With options you can use combination strategies to trade in a flat market. These are crafted Options designed to let you make money when the underlying stock moves either up, down or sideways. Consider this, by cleverly combining Calls and Puts and deploying them to work in harmony you can design strategies whereby:

- You can craft Options that let you profit if the underlying rises or falls, depending on your trading strategy.
- You can also craft Options to make money in sideways moving or flat markets.

Applying options to sector investing

Recently, EFTs' has become a very popular vehicle for options trading because you can design entire diversified portfolios based upon ETFs. Then you can use options to hedge your position or the indeed ensure your entire portfolio.

One of the reasons that EFTs have become so popular is it allows investors to make sector bets without having to get too granular with individual stocks. This is because a strange tendency of the market is that individual stocks do tend to follow the overall direction of the sector's trend. This means you can bet on a sector like Technology without having to research and analyze a particular stock. Also unlike other indexes ETFs are sort of quasi-derivative that you can trade like stocks. That means EFTs can be traded at any time during market hours instead of waiting until the market closes, like you have to do in trading traditional mutualfunds.

Importantly the popularity of ETFs means that they are now offered as listed options – standard options offered on the exchange. That means you can trade options on the underlying ETF just like they were stock. This allows you to diversify and lets you make index bets without using indexoptions. There are also ETFs available that are based on commodity indexes which let you participate in trading commodities without having to trade in futures. The proliferation of EFTs has added an extra dimension to options trading which has inspired innovative trading strategies and tactics.

There are many types of options and many strategic uses for them, but this book concentrates on listed stock options which trade on exchanges. These options are used to manage your risk by limiting your losses but they also offer you the opportunity to speculate for profit when deployed using the correctstrategy.

A Deeper Dive into Options

Options trading has a fearsome but ill-deserved reputation for high risk and complexity but to make the most out of options trading, it's simply necessary that you understand the Option's mechanisms and underlying asset's behavior. Having expertise in the underlying financial instrument whether that is stocks or EFTs goes a long way in mitigating most of the risks and optimizing the potential rewards.

Understanding Option Contracts

We can best consider that a financial option is simply a contractual agreement between two parties. However there are some options contracts that are considered to be over the counter, this is a term that means that they are private agreements between two parties that are not conducted via a trading exchange. This book is about standardized contracts known as listed options that trade on exchanges. Options contracts give the owner certain rights and the seller of the options specific obligations. Here are some of the important definitions and details:

- Call option: A call option provides the holder of the call optionwith the right but no obligation to buy a number of shares, typically 100, of the underlying stock at a specific price by a specific date. By buying a call option the holder gets the opportunity to profit from price gains in the underlying stock during the period that the option is valid at a fraction of the cost of owning the stock.

- Put option: Put options provide the holder the right to sell a specific number of shares, typically 100 of the underlying stock at a specific price by a specific date. Put options are used in bear markets where the prices are falling so Option holders are looking for the prices to fall. Option writers however can use Put options to generate income from those seeking insurance or to acquire stock at favorable prices. This is because Put Options let you profit from a decrease in the underlying stocks price much the same as selling stocks short but at a fraction of the risk.

- Rights of the owner of an options contract: A call option provides the holder the rights to buy a specific number of shares of the stock -typically a contract equates to 100 shares - at a predetermined and locked-in price known as the strike price. On the other hand the holder of a put option has the right to sell a specific number of shares of stock at a predetermined price known as the strike price.

- Obligations of an options seller: Sellers (writers) of Call options have the obligation to sell a specific number of shares, typically 100, of the underlying stock at a predetermined price also known as the strike price. Sellers (writers) of Put options have the obligation to buy a specific amount of stock, typically 100, at a predetermined price known as the strike price.

Options are extremely flexible and can be used for many purposes some of the common usages of stock options is for the following objectives:

- To benefit from bull markets and upward price moves using less money

- To profit from bear markets and their downward price slides without the risk of short selling the stock
- To protect stock or a portfolio from falling prices and sudden market downturns

But Options can have teeth and you must always be aware of the risks of trading options. In order to do so safely you must understand two key concepts:

The first is that Option contracts have a limited life as each contract will have an expiration date. What that means is that you must anticipate the timing of any market movement and not just the direction. Because, should the price-shift you have forecast in a certain stock and in a certain direction does not occur by the expiration date, the Option will be effectively worthless and you will lose your premium.

Therefore it is vital that you become comfortable in making not just directional forecasts but also predictions that are time relevant. This is not as obvious or easy as it may first seem. For example, it's not enough that you forecast and are confident that Apple stock will rise to $175 you need to anticipate when this would happen. The difference in premium prices between a one week or six-month Options will be considerable – so you need to get the timing right to both to avoid losses and optimize profits. The key to this is identifying probability – getting the percentages on your side of the deal.

You are best adjusting to this added criterion by participating in trading Options through paper trading to begin with. This point cannot be reiterated enough for beginners – before you risk your money practice strategies and get a feel for the way the market move with regards time and before you do it in live trading.

Setting your Strategy

Setting the wrong strategy can lead to poor trades and missed opportunities. This can take the form of being over-extended in any individual position or by not recognizing a good trade when you see it. A good strategy will not just help you with trade allocation of funds but in spotting good trades. No strategy can eliminate risk but you can manage risks through a sound strategy. On the contrary a risky strategy will expose you to the possibility of you losing or missing trades and ultimately losing your capital. A good strategy will dictate the principles on which your trading philosophy will be founded.

Option Pricing

A significant part of the learning process when trading Options is recognizing your risks and rewards. They come from how well you understand the value of your Option. However to do that requires that you know how an Option derives its value and what conditions will affect any movement in its price. In order to value an option, you will need to know the following:

- The type and strike price of the option (put or call)
- The price of the underlying security
- The trading volatility in that Option
- The probability of success with that Option
- The trading pattern characteristics of the underlying security for example is it trading volumes steady or volatile
- The time remaining until the option expires

- Knowing your rights and obligations as an option holder or writer

Contract Types: the Calls and Puts

There are basically only two kinds of options: calls and puts. By holding a call you have certain specific rights to buy the stock at a pre-specified price by a certain date. On the other hand, owning or holding a put gives you the holder the right to sell a certain stock at a specific price to the option writer by a certain date. The fundamental difference between a put and a call is that Put option price goes up when the price of the underlying security falls. On the other hand Call option prices go up when the underlying security's price rises. When you hold options, you can assert your rights in your own time and at your own discretion. So, anytime between buying an option and its expiration date, you can either:

- Sell the option prior to expiration.
- Manually exercise it prior to expiration.
- Let it expire for either no value (for a loss) or for value (automatic exercise on your behalf if it is in the money).

As an option writer or seller, you will be obligated to honor a specific set of requirements. What is more, your obligations are out with your control. As the Option holder can exercise their rights at any time before the expiry date. In fact, selling options will give you fewer choices, and the active choices available to you are heavily influenced by the markets. As the expiration date nears, you can either:

- Buy the option back for a profit.
- Buy it back for a loss.

46

- Let the option expire with no value (which will be a profit for you).

Understanding Leverage

A very attractive characteristic of Options is its inherent usage of a thing called *Leverage*. With standard stock trading you would need to buy or sell stock at the market value but that is limited by your funds. So for most beginners and retail traders with only say a $5000 trading fund this means that buying and selling premier stock such as Apple or Amazon is out of the question as it is simply too expensive.

However with Options you are not buying the stock you are buying a contract that gives you the right but not the obligation to buy hence the price and the investment is much lower. But interestingly, the fact that you do not own the stock doesn't prevent you from speculating against it. As one contract will typically consist of 100 shares this provides tremendous leverage as you can reap the benefit in trading in 100 Amazon shares for a fraction of the actual stock price.

Hence, we can say that Options contracts allows the buyers and sellers to make almost the same dollar profit for a much lower financial stake than they could by trading in the actual underlying stock. However, there is as always a big catch as increased leverage proportionately increases risk so just as it can increase profits it also significantly amplifies losses.

Here is an example of how it works in practice: If we consider the earlier Microsoft example, if you speculate that the Microsoft stock will go up in price, you have a couple of options, a) could buy some shares in their stock but if the stock is at $43 per share, it would cost $4,300 to buy 100. If you have limited funds then that might not be feasible. But you could also use plan b) whereby you buy an option to buy 100 shares with a *strike price* of $45 for a premium of $0.13 each, a total of $13.

Now we have to contemplate the potential outcomes of these actions as they are quite different. For example, should the stock increase in price from $43 to $45. Then plan A – where you invested in stock - would reap the benefits of a $200 (less the commissions) profit. But plan B, where you bought an Option with a strike price of $45 you would find that your option is out of the money it did not reach its target, so you can't exercise it as it is worthless.

However, if the stock price rises higher than $45, then the option will become much more profitable. We can demonstrate this by considering that at a stock price of $47, the stockholder has a profit of $400:

> $4,700 − $4,300 = $400 but for a percentage return of $400 ÷ $4,300 = 9.3 percent

The option holder would have a profit of $200:

> $4,700 − $4,500 = $200 at exercise, but the percentage return would be $200 ÷ 13 = 1,538 percent.

As can be seen the option holder received a greater percentage return on their investment on a smaller amount of initial capital.

But what if Microsoft falls in price to $40? The stockholder has lost $4,300 − $4,000 = $300. Unfortunately for the Option holder their option would expire worthlessly, so the option holder spent $13 for 100 options that are now worth nothing but their losses are fixed at $13 dollars regardless of how low the underlying stock may fall.

There are four key differences between trading using the stock position versus the option position:

- The Option strategy costs $13 upfront and the Stock position costs $4,300.
- The stock hold position can lead to larger losses if the position moves against the stock.
- The Option position is higher risk but has fixed maximum losses
- The greater potential for return comes with higher risk.
- With the options strategy, you have an increased percentage return because you earn almost the same dollar profit as you would on the stock position as you are investing less money. Of course, that assumes your option can be exercised. Otherwise, there is no profit only the entire loss of the investment.

Options for Speculation

Leverage, makes Options a very attractive way to speculate in the market. Using this technique Traders are betting using low stakes on price changes that can generate large profits. Of course, making large profits also means taking on large risk hence Options poor reputation as being a high-risk tool for financial trading.

Nonetheless, The Options Exchange works because there are always sufficient buyers and sellers to meet the market demand of those wishing to speculate and those in the market to hedge their positions. Therefore there is always a need for those selling and those buying Options in order to make a functional market. Therefore there is always a need to bring together those looking to hedge and those looking to speculate.

Marking to Market and Margin

As we have seen an attractive feature of Options is that they have built-in leverage. The problem is though that there have to be some controls in place to ensure traders are solvent and able to meet their obligations. If not traders could merrily write Options and rake in premiums as a stream of income without any way of paying up should the market go against them. Therefore, there has to be a way for the exchange to ensure everyone can pay up if necessary when the order to exercise a position is triggered on an expiry date.

Now some of the safeguards to prevent insolvent trading are that you can't place an options trade unless you have money in your account. This is known in broker jargon as a margin. A margin account is the collateral that is used to fund your trading obligations. The amount you require to hold in your broker account will typically be a percentage of your commitments but the exact percentage vary. Also the percentage will vary depending on the type of contract in question. For example if you are writing a contract and hence have an obligation to buy a stock should an Option be exercised the amount you will need to hold in the account will be larger than a trader operating mostly on call options. But it is very complex to place a figure on the monetary value of a position as it depends on the relationship between the income received through writing the option, the inherent value of the option, and the most subjective component being the likelihood of the option being exercised. Remember the vast amount of Options will never be exercised.

Because of this complexity in working out a safe margin, the CBOE provides a margin calculator online at cboe.com/tradtool/mcalc/

The calculator will let you work out just how much cash and other collateral you must keep in your trading account to cover obligations in different trading scenarios.

However it is not just down to the brokers to police their clients' trading accounts as the options clearinghouse - which oversees the transaction between brokers and the exchange and manages the money transactions between parties on behalf of the exchange – will each evening check the value of every account relative to the value of its option position. This is a process known as marking to market.

Marking to market determines if you have enough margin to support your position. If they determine that you have sufficient margin then you are free to continue trading. However should they determine that you have the insufficient margin to cover your obligations you will receive a margin call. This is basically a demand from your broker for more funds to be deposited in your account. If you are not in a position to comply with the demand and are not able to put additional funds into the account to cover your position then your position will be sold.

Chapter 4–Getting to grips with the Jargon

In the first 3 days we have covered a lot of ground regarding Trading Options and are now well on our way to having a good solid foundation for build our trading knowledge. You have learned a lot of the theory and concepts that underpin options trading but before we move on to some of the more advanced practical stuff we have to get to grips with the trading jargon. The problem is that financial trading is steeped in jargon and unfortunately options' trading is no exception to this. Indeed because it is much more complex than the other forms of financial trading it is possibly even more afflicted by the use of strange terms such as moneyness – yes- that is supposedly a word – and we even have a basket full of Greek terms to understand. Unfortunately, if we don't spend the time becoming familiar with the terms now it will make understanding the more advanced concepts we will learn in the next few days almost impossible.

In this Chapter

We will learn:

- The technical terms for the Option variables
- What are the different Puts and Calls
- What are long and short positions
- Why and how do we use long or short on Calls or Puts?
- Writer and Buyers
- Setting the Strike Price
- Understanding the expiration date and process
- Understand the Option styles

Option Contract Variables

So far we have only considered Options as being a contract – but we have not considered many of the confusing terms that are associated with Options. In this section we will dive deeper into the Option contract and try to explain some of the often confusing jargon.

Here are several key terms you have to know in order to make good options trading decisions:

- **Underlying security:** The underlying stock that you buy or sell and that determines the inherent value of the option.

- **Strike price:** The price you would pay per share if you decided to exercise your rights as for call option buyer. For put option buyers it's the price you would receive for exercising and selling stock.

- **Expiration date:** The date the option and your rights disappear.

- **Option deliverable:** The number of shares and the name of the underlying security that you can call away or put to someone.

- **Market quote:** The most current price of an option that is being bid on by buyers and offered by sellers of options.

- **Multiplier:** This is the variable used to determine the value of the option and how much money you will pay it is based upon the number of shares in a single contract. Typically stock options deliver 100 shares per contract, so the multiplier of a per-share option market price and strike price quotes is 100.

- **Premium:**This is the term used to relate to the total value of the option you buy or sell. Thepremium is determined based on the market quote of the option and its multiplier (100)

Listed Options

In general terms a *financial option* is a contractual agreement between two parties. Options can be personalized agreements between two private individuals and these are known as over-the-counter options. However, options traded on exchanges in Options trading are standardized contracts known as *listed options.*

Option contracts have a few characteristics that we must be aware of when beginning trading. For example they have a limited lifetime determined by the expiry date. The expiry date is hugely important because once a contract expires it becomes worthless. What this means is that if you don't exercise your rights on or before the expiry date they will expire and you will lose your premium along with the entire value of the Option. This may well be what you intended as many Options are bought as insurance cover for that time period. However you would not want to lose out on a valuable Option with inherent profit just because you forgot to exercise your option on the correct date. Fortunately many online broker platforms will track and notify you well in advance of any options due to expire so that shouldn't be the problem it once was.

We use stock options for the following objectives:

- To benefit from the leverage that allows us to profit from large stock movements using less money

- To benefit and gain profit from a bear market when there are a downward trend and falling prices in stocks without the risk of short selling
- To protect the overall value of a stock portfolio against persistent falling prices orsudden market downturns

To accomplish these tasks there are fundamentally two main categories of Options - Puts and Calls.

Long and Short Puts and Calls

In general terms an option will give you the right to buy or to sell an asset. Thus there are two main types of options - *call* and *put* – whereby the call gives you the right to buy, and the put gives you the right to sell.

An important thing to understand is the difference between Buyers and Sellers as this is fundamental to the way Options work. The Rights of the owner of an options contract is dependent on the type of contract:

- A call option gives the holder (owner) the right to buy the stock before or at an agreed date at a locked in price. A put option gives the owner the right to sell a specific number of shares of stock at a locked in price.
- Option writer or seller obligations: The writer or sellers of call options have the obligation to sell shares of the underlying stock at the agreed locked in price. Sellers of put options has the obligation to buy from the option holder the pre-agreed amount of stock at the locked in price.

To see how this works in practice let us consider why traders buy call options. Traders will buy call options when they predict an upwards or bull market, i.e. they forecast that stocks will go up

Options Trading Simplified

in price. This is because the call option gives them the right to buy the shares at a lower price than they would otherwise. Now that is straightforward enough, but why do they buy put options? Traders will buy put options when they expect the market to go down, i.e. they will be buying options when they expect a downward trend in the market.

Going long or going short

Another confusing term for beginners and especially those familiar with other stock trading methods is the trading terms, long and short. In general trading terms to take a *long* position is to buy to own it, and to take a *short* position is to sell it.

Nonetheless in Options trading these terms take on more nuanced meanings. In Options trading, the terms of *long* and *short* are more complicated because you are also dealing with whether they are related to puts or call options.

For example, to demonstrate the difference:

- If you take a long position on a call option then you are betting that the price of the underlying asset will rise.
- If you take a long position on a put you are betting on the underlying asset price going down.
- If you are short on a put, you are betting that the price of the underlying asset will be above the strike price.
- If you are short a call, you are also betting that the price of the underlying asset will be below the strike price.

Let's look at some sample transactions.

Trading Long on a Call

If a Trader speculates that a company ABC's stock will be trading above $40 at expiration, which is within a month. The best premium for each Call option with a $40 strike price is $0.85.

Now, if ABC is trading at $45 at the expiration date then all is well and the trader can exercise the option and buy shares at $40 each, for a profit of $5 less the $0.85 premium - $4.15. But if ABC's stock price has remained at or around $40 or less, then the Trader is out the $0.85 option meaning they have lost $0.85x100 =$85.

Trading short on a Call

Another use of a call can be demonstrated when a Trader thinks Company ABC stock will be trading below $50 at expiration date in a months' time. However in this scenario the premium for each call option with a $50 strike price is $2.00. What the Trader can do is writes (shorts) call options at the $50 price and they will receive $2 for each option.

If the price of Company ABC stock at expiration is $40 or below, the Trader is successful and gets to keep the $2 premium per option.

However If the price goes up to say, $54, the Trader will lose $54 − $50 = $4 per share; however the $2 premium offsets half the total loss to $2.

Trading long on a Put

In a third scenario we can see another way of using options when another Trader is confident that Company XYZ stock will be trading below $30 per share at expiration, in 3 months they use a put option.

The premium for a put option with a $30 strike price is $0.75.

If all goes as expected and the price of Company XYZ stock at expiration is $27, then the Trader will make $30 − $27 = $3 per share, less the $0.75 premium for a profit of $2.25.

However, should the price at expiration be $31 or higher, then the Trader is out of the money and the premium for a loss of $0.75.

Trading short on a Put

Another Trader thinks Company XYZ stock will be trading above $70 per share at expiration.

The premium for a put option with a $70 strike price is $1.02, so the Trader writes options at $1.02 each.

At expiration, the stock is at $72 per share, so the Trader gets to keep the $1.02 premium per share.

However, if the stock were to go to $68, then the Trader would then lose $68 − $70 per share, plus the $1.02 premium for a loss of $0.98.

The following table gives you a short summary of what happens to different types of options positions as the underlying asset's price changes.

Basic Put and Call Matrix

Option	Stock Price Goes Up	Stock Price Goes Down
Long call	Profit	Worthless
Short call	Loss	Keep the premium
Long put	Worthless	Profit
Short put	Keep the premium	Loss

Writers & Buyers

The trader who decides to short an option—in effect, sell it to someone else—is also known as the *writer*. For every trade that is made there is a writer and a buyer. Exchanges need both buyers and writers to create the market depth. This is simply because writers construct options to sell to those in the market to buy. In every trade the option writer goes short, and the buyer goes long. Nonetheless, the interesting thing is that even if every trader in the market had a common perception of a stock's behavior, there will still be those that go short when the market as a whole is going long.

The reason for this is that there are always those trading for the purpose of speculation and those looking for insurance. These traders have conflicting interests and objectives so will have to take contrary positions in order to achieve their goals.

For example, Options that are bought for insurance purposes will take the opposite perspective of the market trend. This is because an investor holding a valuable asset for example 100 Apple shares may want them to go up in price but will still need protection against their price falling. Hence the need for a put

Options Trading Simplified

Option with a low strike price that will counter-balance any sudden decline in value.

It is this ability to mix and match long and short, puts and calls in a few different ways that are the foundation in developing options trading strategies and cycles.

Setting the Strike Price

The *strike price* of an option is the predetermined and locked-in price where the option can be exercised at any time up until expiration. For example, a call with a strike price of $70 can be exercised if the underlying price is at $70 or above. At exercise, the trader who wrote the call will receive $70 per share in exchange for a share of the stock. If the trader does not own the stock – remember they do not have to – the required stock will have to be purchased at market price. Whatever, the trader who bought the call has the right to buy the underlying for $70, whether it's worth $70.01 or $876 dollars in the market. The Option writer is obliged to sell the stock at $70 regardless of whether he has to go out to the market and buy it at $70.01 or $876 dollars in order to fulfil the contract.

Similarly, a put option with a strike price of $40 can be exercised if the underlying price is $40 or less. At exercise, the trader who wrote the put will have to buy the stock at $40 per share, whether it is worth $39.99 or $0.00. The holder of the option will receive the difference between the market price and the exercise price.

The following table shows what happens when a call or put expires in the money—that is, when the market price is above the strike price for a call or below the strike price for a put.

	Holder	Writer
Call	Receives cash or security	Delivers cash or security
Put	Delivers cash or security	Receives cash or security

You'll notice that the receiver and deliverer are different for puts and calls, holders and writers. This allows for the structure of many different strategies.

To exercise an option, the holder notifies their broker which then notifies the market clearinghouse, which then in turn notifies the seller that it is time to settle up.

Expiration Date

The *expiration date* is not as straightforward as you might suspect albeit it does mean the day the option is no longer valid. However the way the date is determined is by the month on the contract and the day is the third Friday of the month. Thus an Option will be dated 2019 Dec and the expiry date will be the date on the third Friday of December 2019. By the expiry date the holder must either exercise their rights and the writer has to settle up by that date, or the option will expire and become worthless.

American and European Options

There is some ambiguity between Options as there are two distinct styles an American and a European style. The only real difference but it is a significant one is that an *American option* gives the holder the right to exercise the option at any time after the sale and before the expiration date. On the other hand, a *European option* can only be exercised on the expiration date.

Options Trading Simplified

This is a major difference in terms of trading so you must make sure you know which option style you are trading in.

To compound the problem exchanges issue both types, it is no longer the case that American exchanges only issued American style Options and European only issued European style options now there is a mixture of both. You need to know which you are trading as it can have a large effect of the Options value and ability to be traded.

Chapter 5 - Understanding and Placing Orders

The past 4 days of your journey to becoming an Options trader has been a hard slog as we have struggled to come to terms with the theory and underpinning concepts that support options trading. However, it is all downhill from here. It doesn't get any easier I'm afraid, but it does become more practically orientated as we finally learn how to trade in Options. So in this chapter on our 5th day we will start to pore over and study quote reports and option chains.

The option quote reports and the option chains we use in this section can be accessed at http://www.cboe.com/delayedquote/detailed-quotes?

In This Chapter

We will learn

- How to read option quotes
- To decipher option chains
- Understand option premiums
- learn how to make orders
- Learn the different types of order and when to use them
- Managing margin through the mark to market
- How to open and close an order
- About all the different types of orders and when to use them

Now that you have learned all about the trading concepts behind Options, as well as all the basic terminology, what they are, how they work and why we use them, it's time to get into the details of how options work in an exchange environment. After all Listed Options are sold around the world on exchanges, which may have different rules. Also the Option contracts may have different specifications; they may be American or European style. Therefore, it is very important for you to check the style format and the specific rules for trading in each contract with your broker or the exchange. Most modern broker platforms automatically furnish you with the relevant information as well as track Option expiry dates – as last trading days may differ – but if you are not sure check with the exchange as that at least ensures you won't be unpleasantly surprised.

Nonetheless, despite there being some difference from region to region there is a still far more common ground between exchanges. This is because trading has become electronic and global so there has essentially been a harmonization of different options, trading rules across the different exchanges.

Reading the Quotes

The first thing as a beginner trader that you will need to become familiar with is the confusing and somewhat intimidating dashboard of your online trading app. The broker app that you subscribe to will present you with a digest of the current Options quotes available presented in what is termed quote tables. These tables display a list of option price quotes but they are also crammed with other supporting information. For example they will list the time to expiry, the strike price and the price of the option including the bid-ask spread. These quote tables as they are known will also include information on indicators for the current open interest and the implied volatility.

These price quote tables list what is known in trading as the *options chain* or *options series,* which is the technical term for a list of all of the options currently available for a particular expiration date. However, they are not quite the same thing, as an options chain is a list of all the options available on a specific stock whereas an options series is a list of all the puts and calls on a specific stock that have the same strike price and expiration date.

Nonetheless the terms do appear to be used interchangeably depending on the broker application.

In the following screenshot you can see a quote table with an option chain with the same expiration date but a variety of available strike price.

Calls									03/15/2019
Last	Net	Bid	Ask	Vol	IV	Delta	Gamma	Int	Strike
3.85	+1.27	3.8	3.95	11,655	0.1951	0.8643	0.0677	16975	AAPL 177.500
1.91	+0.745	1.91	1.99	61,903	0.1956	0.6227	0.1178	45939	AAPL 180.000
0.75	+0.345	0.73	0.75	58,877	0.1997	0.3258	0.1094	15035	AAPL 182.500
0.25	+0.125	0.25	0.27	53,371	0.2177	0.136	0.0608	18670	AAPL 185.000

Reading the Quote Table

If we look at the table and read it from left to right we can consider each column in turn:

- Last: This is the price of the last transaction i.e. the latest successful bid price
- Net: This is the change in price between the latest and the price at closing the previous day.
- Bid: This is the highest bid price, which is the highest available price bid by someone to buy the stock.

- Ask: This is the lowest ask price, the best available offer of a price that someone has made to sell the stock
- Bid-Ask spread: Although not shown in our table – we have to calculate it ourselves – this is the difference between the two prices i.e. the lowest ask and the highest bid. The spread is a good indicator or volatility and marker depth as a stock being aggressively traded by many participants will have a smaller spread. Conversely a stock that has low trading volatility and volume with only a few people actively trading will have a higher spread. The bid-ask spread is an important indicator for setting entry and exit price strategies and what type of order to use – i.e. don't use market orders on high spreads use a limit order. The reverse strategy holds true for small spreads. Typically avoid stock with spreads higher than 5-10% as you will likely be overpaying and risk not finding a buyer when it comes to selling.
- Volume: This is the number of trades carried out on the option during the current trading session and this total is reset at the end of every trading day– the higher the volume the more liquid the stock and the better for trading.
- Open Interest: In the option chain this is an indicator – not a live metric - of the number of open options available as it is tallied up at the end of each trading day – higher open interest is an indicator of high trading interests as options are created and retires due to market supply and demand.
- IV: This is termed Implied Volatility (IV) and is an estimate of the trading volatility on that option. You want to buy options when implied volatility is low as options are likely to be at their cheapest due to lower demand and

be an option seller of options when implied volatility is high when options are likely to be more expensive due to higher market demand.

- Delta: Delta is an indicator of the option's sensitivity to changes in the underlying stock price. It provides an estimate of the price change of the option given a $1 change in the underlying stock. So if an option has a delta of 0.2 then for every $1 move in the price of the stock the option price will move $0.20 in the same direction.

- Gamma: This is a measure of how much the delta will change given a $1 move in the underlying stock. Gammas can be thought of as an indicator of the rate of change in delta, so an option with a gamma figure of for example, +0.05 will see its delta indicator value also increase by 0.05 for every $1 movement in the underlying stock price.Gamma is at its highest with at-the-money options and for short-dated options i.e. in the final week. Sellers will want low gamma as they want the prices to stay relatively stable whereas buyers want large gamma as they want prices to rise quickly.

- INT: This is the measure of the Open Interest in that option – in contrast to trading volume – this figure is derived from the previous day's trading

Options Trading Simplified

If we drill down on a quote say for the strike price of $185 we get the detailed price data table shown below:

AAPL190315C00185000   LAST 0.25   CHANGE +0.125 (0%)

Chart

Price Data Table
Mar 12, 2019 @ 22:01 ET   (DELAYED)

Last Sale		0.25	Tick		No_change
Time of Last Sale			Underlying Symbol		AAPL
Net Change		+0.125	Percent Change		0
Previous Close		0.115	Open		0.16
High		0.8	Low		0.15
Bid		0.25	Ask		0.27
Bid Size		1	Ask Size		506
Volume		53,371	Security Type		Option
Open Interest		18670	Expiration Date		03/15/2019

Contract Naming Conventions

Prior to 2010 the standard naming convention for US options was based upon a format where each contract name was made up of the stock's *ticker symbol,* followed by the date of expiration in year/month format, then the type of option – Call or Put, followed by the strike price.

For example: AAPL19MarCall185 was a representation of an option expiring in March 2019 on a Call order for a strike price of $185 and it was very readable but not scalable to the new market volumes. So after 2010 the naming convention and format changed to accommodate scale.

An example of a modern contract name post-2010 would be: "AAPL190315C00185000"

Now let us break this down to show how this equates to March 15th, 2019 $185.00 Call Option on Apple stock.

The new format is 21-bytes long and comprises a (the ticker symbol that indicates the company name) + the Year of expiry (yy) + the Month of expiration (mm) + the actual Day of expiry (dd) + they type of transaction, the Call/Put Indicator (C or P) + Strike Price:

For Example, a March 15th, 2019 $185.00 Call Option on Apple would be listed as "APPL190315C00185000"

What it means:

Component	Value	Location in symbol
Root Symbol	AAPL	AAPL150416C00030000
Expiration Year	2019	YHOO190416C00030000
Expiration Month	03	YHOO150316C00030000
Expiration Day	15	YHOO150415C00030000
Call or Put	Call	YHOO150416C00030000
Strike Price*	$182.00	YHOO150416C00185000

Basics of Orders

Once you decide on a favorable stock and strike price you can browse through the options chain, which will list all the available contracts and their price quotes that meet your criteria. You can choose:

- The contract type

Options Trading Simplified
- Transaction type
- Expiry date
- Strike price

You can scan through the list to find a particular put or a call with a strike price and expiration that you like or you can usually filter only contracts that meet your criteria. Once you have found a contract that matches your requirements you can then place the order.

As we said earlier there is additional support information that is available with each Option. The information will detail such things as the open interest, which will be shown in a column in the quote report showing how many of these contracts are outstanding. Another column of interest indicates the *implied volatility* and this shows the volatility of the price of the underlying asset. If you remember volatility is one of the six factors that determine the valuation of an Option and it is based on the current price of the option.

Option Transactions

There are four basic transactions that make up all Option trading. Even the most advanced trading strategies come down to initiating these four basic transactions to open and close positions. So you must understand their terminology as most transaction will be referred to as one of the following:

- A *buy-to-open* transaction - this gets you a contract to establish a new long position in a put or a call.
- A *sell-to-close* order – this is used to close out or end a position in an existing long contract.

- A *sell-to-open* order – this order is used to write a put or a call and to establish a new short position.
- A *buy-to-close* transaction – this is used to end an existing short position.

Opening and Closing a Position

When you open or enter a position you are actually submitting your order to buy an option. However, when you make your bid there may not be an available option on the market with anyone willing to take the other side of the trade. But you won't know that, because your demand will create a contract if one isn't already in existence with a counterparty willing to take the other side of the trade. Therefore an important factor is in knowing the correct protocol to use when you go about entering and exiting positions.

For example: To buy a call option, the correct protocol for you to use can be seen in the following order:

Buy to Open, 1 APPL March 15 185.00 Strike Call Option

Now to exit that open position, you would then have to submit the following order:

Sell to Close, 1 AAPL March 15 185.00 Strike Call Option

You will use the same type of order and protocol when opening a position in an option with underlying stock that you don't own. This is because the simplicity of the order process only requires that you specify the stock of the option you are selling. Therefore you would use the same protocol and order format when opening and closing an option that you don't own:

Sell to Open, 1 APPL March 15 185.00 Strike Call Option

Buy to Close, 1 APPL March 15 185.00 Strike Call Option

The underlying importance of ensuring a strict protocol is to enable the exchange and clearinghouse to match and tally up the number of transactions at the end of each day. This also allows them to determine the number of open contracts, which is also known as the open interest.

Selling an option you don't own

When you take up a position by writing or selling a call option as an opening transaction, you are now on the opposite side of the deal so you become obligated by market rules to sell a stock at the strike price at any time until the option expires. For the time you sell the option if a call option holder goes in the money and decides to exercise their rights, you the option writer will have to meet your obligation. In trading terms this is called *being assigned* the option. When you are assigned on a call option contract, you will have only a couple of alternatives:

- If you are covered and you own sufficient shares then you must sell the shares to close the position.

- If you are in a naked position then you will need to buy the shares regardless of the cost.

If you own shares when you sell a call option, it is known as a *covered* transaction, because you have the underlying shares to *cover* your short position. However, if you don't own the shares to cover the position when you sell the call, this is known as a *naked call*. You should never as a beginner open a naked call as the losses can be *unlimited* given the market potential of stock to continue to rise indefinitely.

On the other hand if you sell a put option as an opening transaction, you are putting yourself into the position of holding an obligation to buy the stock at the locked in strike price at any point until the option expires. Should anyone exercise their rights you will be assigned the option, and this typically happens on a short put when the underlying stock has fallen. If assigned, you will be obliged to buy stock buying stock at a higher price than the current market value. As with the call option your short put position can be covered if you hold the stock or naked if you have no stock.

Selling puts is a risky transaction not for beginners or the fainthearted, the reason for that is when you sell an option, you are creating a short position on a stock option contract and are effectively out of the active decision-making process. This means you are at risk of assignment from the time you create the position all the way through to the expiration of the contract. The only way you can get out of the obligation is to exit the position. To exit the position means entering a Buy to close order for the option.

Understanding option orders

Options are made on demand by the market and are not limited in the way stock is by its float, which is the term used to describe the number of shares outstanding and available in the market to trade for stock.

 Contracts are different in there is no physical limit as they are created on-demand when two traders create a new position, or open a trade. This increases the metric that is known as open interest for that specific option. Open interest is a measurement of market sentiment for that option and it decreases when traders close existing positions.

Open interest is typically done on a market-wide basis and doesn't get updated trade-by-trade. It's more an end-of-day reconciliation by the Options Clearing Corporation (OCC) as they need to keep the accounting straight and control all that leverage. It also means you'll have to communicate a little more information when placing option orders than trading in stocks.

Knowing basic option order rules

Buying or selling options can be done on any order. However, you cannot just create orders haphazardly as the ability to go long (buy) or short (sell) a contract depends on your brokers' permission. The broker is likely to make their decision based upon your history, experience, trading strategy and the option approval level for your account. This is to prevent beginners or the inexperienced from creating unlimited-risk, short-option positions, which could be calamitous until their broker approves the transaction.

Because contracts are created and retired based on market demand, you must enter orders in a way that supports this end-of-day reconciliation by the options markets. This requires the use of a specific language. For example:

- A new position you're creating is an opening order.
- An existing position you're exiting is a closing order.

Using a call option as an example, the following table provides you with the transactions required to enter and exit a long call or short call position.

Position	Entry	Also Known As	Exit	Also Known As
Long Call	Buy Call to Open	BCO	Sell Call to Close	SCC
Short Call	Sell Call to Open	SCO	Buy Call to Close	BCC

When exercising or getting assigned on an option contract, there is no closing transaction. The same holds true for options expiring worthless. In each case, the appropriate number of contracts is removed from your account after the transaction completes or expiration weekend comes to an end.

Basic Order Types

Before you place an order however you need to understand what type of order you wish to make. You will find that you have a variety of different order types available, some orders are designed to guarantee to fill an order but not necessarily at the price you desired (such as market order) whereas others are configured to guarantee price but not necessarily to fill the order (such as limit orders). Although there are some other unique parameters and considerations for options orders, the fill-versus-price conundrum remains the most common reason for selecting an order type.

By managing the orders behavior means that you have greater control as to how the order is executed as well as the price. When in doubt, consider what limits your risk.

Options Trading Simplified

There are several types of orders that have certain parameters that affect the way they are carried out. These parameters are selectable which allows you to fine control the behavior of the order.

An options transaction can be configured to be executed in a particular way by using parameters the trader sets when the order is placed. Almost all brokerage applications that support the handling and trading of options will allow traders to set these basic parameters. These configurable orders are essential today as market prices fluctuate rapidly due to high volume electronic trading. Therefore as prices change quicker than a human can respond traders need to try and automate the trading processes. By having a good understanding of the types of orders available to you can greatly reduce the stress and the losses associated with financial trading.

Many of these parameters change the order type and its behavior and are required by an average trader as several of the order types are based on prices:

Market orders

Market orders are standard trading orders used to buy and sell at the best price on the exchange when the order is placed. The issue with a market order is it does just that it trades at the best price available which is not always the price you want. Therefore you use a market order when you are more concerned with obtaining or ridding yourself of the stock rather than the price. Market orders are the most common type of orders.

Limit orders

Limit orders are a type of order used to selectively buy or sell only at a specific price or better (higher for a sell order, lower for a buy order). A limit order works just like a market order except that it will only match a trade if the best match also matches the pre-determined price. The broker can only execute the order if the price meets your pre-set price criteria. But limit orders can also work against you if you are not careful. For example, you place a limit order on a call option to buy at $10 when the option is trading at $12, and the price falls to $10.01, your order would not be executed. This behavior may be what you want as the use of Limit orders does make trading more predictable, but they might also lead to missed opportunities.

Generally, limit orders are good for entering a position; this is because you only want to establish positions that are within your desired trading allocations. However, if you need to guarantee an exit, only a market order will guarantee that for you. Effectively managing order execution means knowing when it's more important to get the order executed versus the price where it's executed. When in doubt, consider what limits your risk.

Stop orders

Stop orders are very important and you need to know how they work and practice setting them by paper trading. A stop order is designed to trigger and to buy or sell once an option hits a specific price. Stop orders are typically used to automate trading as they limit losses by closing a position if a particular price is hit. However stop orders should not be confused with limit orders because stop orders are used very differently than limit orders as they continue to be executed if the stop is hit. For example, if you place a stop order of $10 to close out a call position at $10.50, i.e. to limit any losses and lock in the $10 profit. In this scenario the stop order will be executed as soon as the price hits $10. But here is the problem as a stop order reverts then to working as a market order and fills the order with the best available price and that may be $9 so it ends up filling the order at a worse price.

Stop-limit orders

The solution to the fallibility of a standard stop order is to use a stop-limit order, which is a combination of a stop and a limit order. This aggregate order is only executed when the stop price is hit but the order only executes at the limit price or better. The stop-limit order does enforce a level of discipline on the trade but it is however still restricted to only making a trade should there be a matching trade available – which means you might miss the opportunity to abandon a position which can lead to even greater losses.

Placing a stop order is similar to monitoring security and placing a market order when certain market conditions are met. A sell-stop order gets triggered when either the option trades at or below your stop price or if the asking price reaches your stop. On the other hand a buy-stop order gets triggered when the option trades at or above your stop or when the bid price reaches your stop. Because you sell on the bid and buy on the ask prices you will need to account for the bid-ask spread when you are determining an appropriate option stop level. Another issue with option stop orders is duration. The option contract you're trading may only allow day-stop orders so you'll need to enter a new stop order each evening after the market closes.

Stops are superior to stop-limit orders for managing risk because they guarantee an execution if the stop condition is met. Some systems will allow you to have two standing orders for the same underlying stock. If that is the case then include a stop-loss order for the purpose of risk management and a limit order configured for profit-taking. If your platform allows a "one cancels other" trade type, then you can enter both orders that way.

A system that supports a one cancels other order will allow you to enter two different orders that are both active on the same stock in the market. The way it works is that if or when one of those orders is executed, the system will automatically cancel the other order. But be aware if the system doesn't support one cancels other, then having two live orders against the same stock position is dangerous as it would only take a strong swing in the position to cause both orders to trigger and be filled. This could result in you holding an unlimited risk position. Too often beginner traders who fail to grasp the nuances of options stop trades and pay the price for not being diligent in selecting their order types.

In terms of duration, the two primary periods of time your order will be in place are as follows:

- The current trading session or the following session if the markets closed.
- Until the the broker clears the order or the order is cancelled by you
- Order duration is identified by adding day or good 'til cancelled (GTC).

- Market orders guarantee execution, so they are good for the day only.

If you want to cancel an active order, you need to submit a Cancel Order. After the instructions are completed, you receive a report back notifying you that the order was successfully cancelled. It is possible for the order to already have been executed, in which case you receive a report back indicating that it is too late to cancel. One thing to be aware of is that you cannot cancel a market order. This is because it is guaranteed to be filled at the best available price.

You will also find that the way you go about changing an order is a little different from the way that you cancel one. This is becausethere are two ways to change an order:

- Cancel the original order, wait for confirmation of the cancellation, and then enter a new order.
- Submit a Cancel/Change or Replace Order

Even though the electronic order process is very fast, when replacing an order it's better to use the Change/Cancel approach. Otherwise, you must wait for the cancellation confirmation report before you can make your new order so as to avoid duplicating an executed order.

There are other, special purpose order types available that are less used that we will discuss in the next section as it is important to know all the choices you have to hand. This is simply because it is your responsibility to select the correct order type. So it is crucial that you understand all the order types available and how they behave and are handled in the market. What you will find is that the order type when using trading options online, will appear in the order drop-down menu. Here will be all the pertinent choices, and the order ticket will have all the required boxes. Nonetheless you must still read the order ticket carefully before hitting the Execute button. Also read the confirmation ticket that you will receive because if you have accidentally filled in the wrong box you could have committed to a very risky trade.

Type of Order	Guarantees
Market Order	Order will be executed (filled)
Limit Order	Order will get fixed price
Stop Order or Stop-Loss Order	Order will be executed (filled)
Stop Limit Order	Order will get fixed price

Specialist Types of Order

Price is not the only parameter that can be used to tune the behavior of an order as traders can also set time limits on their orders:

- *Day orders* will be executed and filled if possible the same day they are received and are always cancelled at the end of the day if they cannot be filled Day orders are standard orders in day trading
- *Good 'til date (GTD) orders* work in a similar manner but they are good until the end date specified, if they cannot be filled earlier they always terminate on the expiry date.

- *Good 'til cancelled (GTC) orders* are not date dependent and will remain valid until they are filled or until the trader cancels the order.

These are additional parameters that determine stock so in addition to price and time a trader can request All *or* None for the order. How this works is that if a trader makes an order for 3 Options at a defined price they can also set the all or none parameter. This determines how the order will be filled. Without that parameter being set, the trader might receive only one Option i.e. a partial fill, which might not be desirable.

Advanced Order Types

Traders are always on the lookout for more control over their orders. That's especially true in options trading so many brokerage firms will offer additional types of useful orders:

Contingent orders

This type of order can trigger two transactions at the same time. A contingency order can be executed if the underlying or another security reaches a target price. They are sometimes used for placing stop-loss points, as they don't show up in in the order book. This is especially helpful for options traders

Trailing stop orders

These are orders to buy or sell once an option hits a specific price. Unlike stop orders, they are set as a percentage above or below the option's current market price. This means they can be set to move with the market. This prevents the order being triggered when it is no longer advantageous. Further, if the price moves back in a favorable direction, the stop will be automatically reset.

One cancels other (OCO) orders

OCO orders are actually two orders that are placed at the same time with the understanding that if one order's stop price is hit and it is triggered, then the other order will be cancelled automatically. That means they can be used to automatically close positions when either a target profit or loss target is hit.

One triggers other (OTO) orders

OTO orders are another type of combination order whereby two separate orders are placed simultaneously. The goal here is that if one of the orders is triggered then that will cause the other to execute. For example, an OTO can be used as a stop order, which will close one position but also causes another order to be opened automatically.

Chapter 6 – Being in the Money

At the end of day 5 you reached a point whereby you understand all about option theory and how to read a quote table. You know what the parameters and metrics are and how to use them to select attractive options from the options chain. Using this knowledge can assist you in selecting good options that match your specific trading intentions. Furthermore you will now know what type of orders to use and in what scenario. This will enable you to control the price you pay/receive on a transaction or guarantee an entry or exit from a position in a hurry. You will also know how to combine orders to blend custom actions to suit any trading scenario. Now on day 6 we will move on to consider the financial position of an option and whether it is financially attractive, we will also turn to consider entry and exit strategies based upon the financial status of an option.

IN THIS CHAPTER

You will learn:

- All about moneyness
- How to judge whether an option is in, at, or out of the money
- How to choose good entry and exit point in a trade
- How to exercise your right at expiry
- How to evaluate an Option (intrinsic vs. extrinsic value)
- How to gauge the effects of volatility
- How to use the Greeks

The concept of moneyness

The term moneyness is used in Options trading to describe the financial status of an Option. An option is said to be *in the money*— or profitable to exercise if its strike price is lower than the price of the underlying asset. For example it would be in the money if you could exercise your rights to buy the underlying stock at the strike price to immediately sell on the market for a profit.

However, the concept of moneyness has a few different aspects to it.

Remember that the strike price is the locked-in price that the underlying stock can be bought or sold for, if exercised. Therefore the strike price is an important factor in determining the Options value as we can compare the Options strike price with the actual market price of the stock. This relationship between the strike and actual market price determines the intrinsic value of the Option and will be a determining factor:

- At the money: This is when the strike price and the stock price is the same and so it applies to both calls and puts
- Near the money: As it is unlikely for the strike and actual price to exactly match any close to equality is termed near the money
- In the money: This is when the strike price in a call option is below the price of the actual stock. On the other hand with a put option the strike price is in the money when it is above the stock price

- Out of the money: This is when a call option strike price is above the stock price. With a put option the strike price will be out of the money when it is below the stock price

As you start to practice and gain experience working with quote tables and orders, you will become very familiar with these terms. This is because you will soon become accustomed to using the relationship between the stock price and the strike price to determine if there is any intrinsic value in the Option. A thing to remember is that only options that are "in the money" will have any intrinsic value.

Indeed, an option will be said to be *in the money* only if it is profitable to exercise. It is *out of the money* if it is not profitable. This means that just because the strike price is above or below the actual price doesn't automatically make it in the money as we must always consider the cost of the premium. Also, the relationship of the underlying price to the strike price depends on the type of option involved.

In other words, a long call is in the money if the strike price is less than the underlying stock price. Therefore you would make a profit if you to exercise your rights under the option, by buying the underlying asset, and then selling it at the higher market price. On the other hand, if the underlying stock price is less than the strike price, then the option is out of the money.

Conversely for the writer of the option, the trader that is obliged to fulfil the holder's rights whether that is to buy or to sell, then they will have the opposite point of view. For the writer of the Option has taken a short position and will be out of the money when the price of the underlying asset is greater than the strike price and in the money when the price of the underlying asset is less than the exercise.

Similarly, the positions are reversed when we consider relative perspectives of the holder and writer of the put option. For example, if the holder of a put option has a strike price of $35 and if the underlying stock is trading at more than $35, then they would be out of the money as it would not be profitable to exercise, so the long put position would be out of the money. However the holders long put would be in the money if the underlying were to trade at less than $35.

But conversely, if we consider the short put position, we will find that an underlying price of more than $35 would mean the option would not be exercised by the holder, so the writer could keep the premium and be in the money. But, if the underlying stock price were to fall below $35, then the option would be in the money from the holder's perspective as it could be exercised at a profit and the writer's short position would now be out of the money.

The following table offers a neat summary of it all.

The Moneyness of an Option

Position	In the Money	Out of the Money
Long call	Stock > Strike	Stock < Strike
Short call	Stock < Strike	Stock > Strike
Long put	Stock < Strike	Stock > Strike
Short put	Stock > Strike	Stock < Strike

Stock = current market price of the underlying stock (variable)

Strike = the locked-in strike price of the Option (fixed)

As we can see the holder and the writer of the Options always have an opposite position except when the strike price and the underlying price are the same, then the option is *at the money or near the money.* This is regardless of the type of option whether it is a put or a call, or whether you are going long or short.

Furthermore, the moneyness of an option is not affected by the style of the option. What this means is that even with a European option, which can only be exercised at the expiry time, it can still transition many times during that period often jumping between being in, out, or at the money at any given time.

Open Interest

An interesting metric that is often included in quote tables for Option contracts is an indicator depicting Open interest, which is the total number of outstanding options contracts. Open interest is tallied at the end of each day. Open interest is used as a metric for the measurement of market sentiment. It should not be misinterpreted as the number of options traded because it is not the same thing as volume as many options are traded to close out existing positions.

However if you are speculating in short term trading of options then Open Interest is an important metric as you will want as much market interest as you can get on your option. This will make it easier to trade when you choose to exit the position as there will likely be many potential buyers.

Expiration and Exercise

Options expire at regular intervals determined by the expiration date, which is the date the option expires. Most options expire on the third Friday of a given month. However, some high-volume weekly options have expiration dates every Friday. The last time to trade the option is at the close of the market immediately before the option expires. Some European options close earlier (sometimes on a Thursday but the closing time would be specified for the option, and most broker apps track the options expiry dates and send a notification so you'd know):

The option period is the term used to denote the valid time **until** expiration and it starts the moment the option is made (written) and ends on the expiry day. However, there are ways to stay in the position if you want to beyond the expiry date. If you want to maintain the position you can *roll* by closing your current – soon to expire - open position and simultaneously make a new position at a different strike price or expiration.

Exercising your Rights

To *exercise* is the term used to cash in an option but the vast majority of options are never exercised. But should you want to and you have a call option giving you the right to buy shares of ABC at $100 per share, and the stock is trading at $105, all you have to do is notify your broker that you want to exercise the Option.

When exercising your option to buy the stock you will need to have the funds in your account. Almost all brokers will require that you buy – pay for the stock – before you sell. This means that you will need sufficient funds in your account before you can exercise your position. Some brokers allow you to turn around and sell the stock immediately and you may get away with selling the stock before you pay the broker, but that type of free-riding - is frowned up.

Delivery and Settlement

When a call option on a stock is exercised, the writer has to transfer the shares to the option buyer's account at the strike price. If the writer is not covered by already owning the stock they must go and buy the shares in the open market.

However, if there is an option for *cash settlement,* then the person whose option is profitable receives a cash transfer payment. This is more commonly used in trading in index options.

Extrinsic and Intrinsic Value

Options have two primary sources of value. The *intrinsic value* is the option's strike price in relation to the price of the underlying asset. An option has intrinsic value only if it is in the money. If it is not in the money then there is no profit so no value.

Time value, on the other hand is known as *extrinsic value.* This value is the difference between the option's price and the amount of intrinsic value - the amount it is in the money. The logic behind this is that the amount that an option is in the money is its intrinsic value, the profit should you claim it today.

But the option can be worth more today than the profit you would realize if you exercised it. This is an important consideration when you are hedging as you do not want to exercise the option – take the profit. Instead you value the time remaining on the insurance value of the option. This additional time value cannot be ignored as it explains why people will often hold onto options when they are profitable to exercise. Of course they may just be riding a trend and hoping to end up with a larger profit.

Nonetheless, it is important to realize that Options do have both extrinsic value and intrinsic value. The more you understand the components of an option's price, the better you can value the option relative to your needs.

One additional concept of Option value that we must know about is *parity*. When we refer to Parity with regards to an Options value we mean the point where an option is in the money but has no time value. Options generally don't reach parity until just before expiration.

Weighing Option Costs and Benefits

There are many advantages to trading using options, but you don't get all those benefits without taking on-board some element of risk. A notable risk that you have to accept is that options have a limited lifespan as they are limited by an expiry date. Now there are clear strategies that you must have in place when handling this risk such as having an exit strategy. For example your choices are, trade the option during the timespan of the option, expire the option on or before the expiry date or simply let the option expire.

However, there can be a big problem with just leaving options to expire. For example, if the option is in-the-money at expiration, your broker may well automatically exercise/assign the option. The problem here is that by exercising the valuable option they have effectively converted a low-cost option position into a high-cost stock position, which you may not want or be able to afford. Consequently, you need to carefully monitor your options and check for notifications from the broker platform regarding any in-the-money option positions, which are nearing the expiration date. You need to do this in anticipation of this likely change in your margin requirement. Alternatively you want to make sure you have sufficient time to trade the option or make other adjustments such as rolling over a trade in order to avoid buying the stock.

Risk of Leverage

Another significant risk to be aware of is that of leverage. Because Options don't cost much as stock as they are simply a contract, this means that they experience disproportionately larger percentage price gains in reaction to the far more expensive underlying stock's very small price movements. The huge benefit of this is that it results in large percentage gains when the underlying stock moves in the anticipated direction by even a small amount. The downside though is that it also results in a 100% wipe-out of the investment if the stock moves by even the smallest amount in the wrong direction. This is not necessarily an issue with beginners or at least it shouldn't be as the risk manifests itself mainly through trading too large a position size. However, you need to be aware that as beneficial as leverage clearly is, it can also be a double edge sword, so be aware that leverage is a risk that needs to be addressed. One simple way to nullify or minimize this level of risk is to keep your position size small.

Lastly, Options as we know possess a time value (extrinsic value) in addition to their inherent intrinsic value (in the money value), which is also another double-edged sword. For option buyers, time-decay acts as a headwind because it is continually decreasing the value of the option. By doing so this increases the dependency on greater stock price movement to break even on the trade. For option writers, it acts as a tailwind because it allows a profit to be generated through steady premium incomes regardless of whether the stock moves or not.

Two other option cost factors should be considered:

1. Costs associated with the trading process
2. Cost of exercising the stock

By understanding the basic cost structure for an option, you can see how options also add through leverage an element of risk, despite the fact that options also provide leverage at a reduced risk.

To complicate the matter a little is the fact that Option prices are partially based on probabilities. For stock options, you want to consider the likelihood that a particular option will be in-the-money before or at expiration given the type of price movements the underlying stock has recently undergone. The way an Option is valued takes into consideration 6 factors; Stock price, strike price, time to expiration, interest rates and dividends but there is a wildcard factor – volatility.

Understand the role of Volatility

Volatility is often considered to be a wildcard because it is difficult to gauge in real time as it is constantly changing throughout each hour of every trading day. As a result to determine the level of volatility mathematicians have come up with a model that indicates an implied value and it does this by working backwards. How it does this is to use the other known inputs listed above and then subtracts that figure from the current option price being quoted to arrive at the up to date volatility figure.

An interesting thing about options is that although they derive their value from the underlying asset the price is not a fixed 1:1 ratio. For example a $1 dollar movement in the price of a stock does not necessarily result in a similar $1 price move on the option. This is because as we have seen that the option price is determined by several factors such a strike, price, expiry time, volatility, etc. However, the largest single factor in an option's value is the underlying stock's price, so there is a relationship between the two.

In order to work out the relationship mathematicians have developed a set of variables, which traders call the Greeks – delta, gamma, theta, and rho. The Greeks are used to try and understand the relationships and the dynamics between the option and stock prices. These variables are considered to be very important to traders as they need to predict how an option's price may change in response to changes in a stock's price.

Using "Greeks" for Options Trading

The Greeks provide an easy way for traders to predict changes in an options price in response to a price change in the underlying stock. The downside is however that they also add a level of complexity and confusion that is disproportional to the benefit they provide. This is because overwhelmingly the most important factor affecting the value of an option is the difference between the stock price and strike price and the time left before expiry. The other components do affect the option price but to an almost negligible level in comparison. So when using the Greeks try and not get too wrapped up in this fine analysis that you lose sight of what is really important.

The Greeks in Brief

The Greeks are valuable variables that can be helpful to traders and analysts so we provide an overview of what each one aims to measure. In brief, as we have seen already when reading option quote tables, Delta measures how sensitive an option's price is to changes in the underlying stock's price. Gamma is a measure of the rate of change of delta. These two variables are the most commonly used Greeks but there are others. Theta, for example, is a measure of the value decay in an option as it approaches its expiration date. Then there is Vega, which is an indicator of the sensitivity of an option's price to volatility in the stock's price. There is also, Rho which is one of the Greek variables that indicates how an option's price be affected by a change in interest rates.

The Greeks are very important if you wish to take a deeply scientific approach to options trading but for most traders and especially beginners they are more a distraction that can trigger analysis paralysis.

Chapter 7- Trading like a Pro

In this the seventh and final day we will wrap up with a chapter dedicated to helping you take a professional approach to trade in options. We will show you how to run your trading operation as a business by observing the best practices and procedures that the professionals use. We will also set out a good trading strategy that will provide income and profits regardless of the market conditions as well as some specialist strategies that you can use when trading under specific market conditions.

IN THIS CHAPTER

You will learn:

- To Develop a reliable business/trading plan
- Identifying business costs
- Minimizing learning curve costs
- Understanding order execution
- Design a small business strategy
- How to use risk defined or risk capped strategies
- Different types of beginner strategies
- When to use the trading strategies to best effect

Treating Option Trading as a Business

In this chapter we will move on to the management and business skills that you will need to adapt to become a successful Option

97

trader. This is simply because trading options is a business albeit with unique situations but it does require its own management style. No matter what you trade, you are a business manager running a financial trading business. Therefore you must become comfortable understanding the costs associated with operating the business as this help you budget accordingly. In business a simple equation of Profits = Cash Income – Operating Expenses, will dictate how profitable a business is being run. Therefore your goal as a business manager will be to maximize profits and an easy way to do that is control or minimize operating expenses.

Now as a beginner, operating expenses may be high as initially certain costs will be unavoidably higher. This is because you will likely be paying more for a broker platform, education and your trading losses. But that's all part of the learning curve that any beginner must expect when they start trading. However, as you become more experienced and your trading skills and strategies evolve, many of those starter costs will go down. However as you get more experienced you will start to realize the need for more complex strategies and market analysis tools so subscriptions to analysis platforms and data services will likely go up.

Nonetheless, always keep in mind that Option trading for you is a business and that some early losses are part of those operating expenses. The goal of course should be to manage the risk and thereby minimize it but the nature of trading makes it impossible to eliminate risk. Managing risk is very doable and is done by disciplines fund management through determining proper trade allocation amounts and setting maximum loss per trade.

Starting out you should never be risking more than 1%-3% of your fund on any one trade. Options trading is far more flexible than most other types of financial trading in allowing this due of course to the lower prices and the power of leverage. And although effectively executing trades is one way of minimizing losses, designing reliable fund management and a trading plan is the foundation of a successful trading career, which will be judged on longevity.

Controlling your emotions

It one thing being keen and wager to start trading but it's quite another to start to trade without a deep understanding of what you are actually doing. If for example you just jump in with little market knowledge you will be gambling using your limited knowledge. This can lead to emotional trading whereby you can start reacting to price movements in an irrational manner. Humans are after all irrational creatures and we tend to stick with something long after we should have chucked it as a bad deal. This is a form of what is called cognitive bias which leads us to continue to throw good money after bad because we think we must turn around our losses. The problem is that emotional trading is usually the path to even bigger losses. That's why we have to understand the rules about sunk costs – went it's lost it is lost, forget it and move on. When we have strict rules that free us from chasing losses and allow us to let go we can then start to consider each trade as a separate entity with no correlation or connection with anything that has gone before. Then we can start to trade rationally and logically. And this is why you need to design an anticipatory trading plan.

A suitable trading plan should have these basic ingredients:

- That you have the technology that you need to trade efficiently such as a computer, fast internet and mobile devices that will allow you to work anywhere
- Time Management: You need to plan your working hours so that you can commit time to trading. Short term positions will require more of your time so allocate the hours necessary to monitor your trading position
- Good Communication: Build up and have to hand a collection of reliable and trusted real-time quote tableand option chain services.
- Reliable Trade Execution: Work with an online broker that has a good reputation for efficiently and accurately executing trades.
- Education: A trading plan must take into account provisions for developing your skills. This should include working on enhancing your technical and fundamental analysis skills. You will also need to develop good option chain and chart reading skillsin order to find appropriate options and opportunities.

Managing Your Costs

There will be a variety of start-up and operational costs that you will need to consider when starting your trading business. But after saying that there will be expense categories that will persist throughout your trading career:

- Education: Training expenses will include materials, courses, and of course the unavoidable learning curve losses when trying new strategies and tactics as well as when entering new stocks in the market. Some of the learning costs will hopefully decrease as you hone your skills and find the strategies and tactics that work for you, but other will persist as you will need to stay abreast of developing market conditions.One of the most enduring costs of trading will besupporting your learning curve. This would hopefully decline as your experience and knowledge grow but you will need to come to terms with the following:

- o Trade in the best conditions for each type of option, stock and strategy.
- o Select options with the appropriate liquidity.
- o Develop your paper-trading and chart reading skills.
- o Manage your fund by allocating the appropriate amount to each trade.
- o Effectively enter orders for the best exit.
- o Take profits.

- Analysis costs: As you progress from a beginner concentrating primarily on long call options and your skills progress you will naturally become more adventurous. Further, as your trading generates regular profits, you may start to migrate to more advanced and risky strategies. To successfully manage this trading transition will place a heavy emphasis on adding analytical tools to your business costs. Analytical tools for deep technical analysis are one of the few costs that may increase as your skills develop.
- Trading costs: One of the most easily forgotten or commonly overlooked costs is brokerage fees for handling the transaction or exercising the option. You need to

calculate them into all calculations when determining if the position is in the money or not. Many beginners remember and account for the commission but forget to consider for slippage. Slippage is the cost associated with the market spread — it is the difference between the bid and the ask prices and that is where the broker makes their profit. A good exercise to get you familiar with your broker's charges is to paper trade using commission and slippage percentages for different size option positions. Soon you will have a feel for what the charges will likely be for different price points such as $1, $5, and $10.

- Taxes are another consideration and you can get the full information from the Internal Revenue Service (IRS) (www.irs.gov).

- If you open a margin account whereby you borrow from your broker you need to add that monthly margin interest fees into the calculation. As a beginner you should not need to do this but as you get more skilled you may start to use short option positions, which will have margin requirements. If you decide to write short option strategies that will be requiring margin, be sure you fully understand all of the associated fees and account charges.

- Losses are another trading cost you could say it is an occupational hazard. Nonetheless losses have to be considered part of doing business. They are certainly likely to be higher at first, but can be reduced but never eliminated altogether through diligent paper trading and experience.

As you spend more time trading and get sufficient time and experience under your belt you will find that sticking to your trading plan will help keep these initial costs to a minimum. Some important factors to bear in mind are:

- Determining the trading allocations: The term trading allocation means the safe amount relative to your capital fund that you can risk on a single trade. Hence a crucial element of a trading plan should identify both your total trading capital as well as your maximum amount, the allocation, that you are willing to risk per trade. Of course if you are experienced in other forms of financial trading such as direct stock and ETF trading you will know that they will require larger risk or per trade funding than when trading positions in options. If you are trading on limited funds then you may if you are risk averseset a maximum allocation amount for every new strategy, say 1% to 3% of capital funds. However that should be based on your paper-trading results and you should always avoid over-committing funds to a single trade.
- Calculate the trade size: You must also determine guidelines for maximum position size prior to entering any trade. It is important to always identify beforehand the maximum number of contracts you can take on a position. The way to do this is to divide the option price by the allocation amount that you are comfortable with and ensure it is below your maximum limit. It is best not to try to use the max allocation as that can be very risky should the trade turn against you.
- Identify the maximum acceptable loss on a trade: When you contemplate this figure it is essential that you control your greed or fear. Consequently, you should set the maximum acceptable loss that you are comfortable with at either a pre-defined dollar value or an as a percentage or the return on investment (ROI). The latter metric may be preferable because a fixed dollar amount can be

Options Trading Simplified

significant only if you are trading with larger allocations than on smaller trades in less liquid stocks.Of course success in percentage gains does not put food on the table or bolster your trading account only dollar gains does that. Either way you should regularly check your trading performancethrough an analysis on your trade results. This is essential in determining if your strategy is correct and that your losses remain at acceptable and ultimately sustainable levels. Even a brief periodic review of your trading results should be enough to let you know how well you are doing. After all you must know how much money you are gaining or more importantly if there is sufficient capital left in your trading account and whether the strategy is working.

- Focus on entry and exit rules: The decisions to enter into an Option position come about by spotting trending market conditions but they may also be based around a scheduled event. In which case the Option exits will tend to be after the scheduled event has passed. The may alsobe triggered by a change around in a market trend. Regardless, of the reason why you enter or exit a position they must be consistent with your overall risk management strategy that determines the maximum acceptable loss per trade.

- Exiting a position based on technical indicators alone will not enable you to take an acceptable loss metric into the equation.Therefore you will need to come up with your own figure for an acceptable loss and set your stop loss orders to match

- It is always a good business model to segregateyour brokerage account used just for options trading from other trading interests. This could make your record keeping and your life much simpler.

Optimizing Order Execution

Successfully trading options means gaining proficiency with order execution. A variety of factors come into the mix here:

- Understanding order placement rules unique to options
- Knowing how different order types work
- Learning how to use combination orders for multi-leg positions
- Gaining skill while using the underlying to identify option exists
- Recognizing your broker's role in execution quality

There is also a learning curve for executing options trades, but for the most part these are mechanical steps that can be easily mastered with some practice. You can get a leg up on this with your paper trading, but it's never the same as the real-time action. This will go a long way toward successful strategy implementation.

Trading rules you should know

Whenever you begin trading a new market, you'll need to become acquainted very quickly with the trading rules. Usually your broker or their trading platform will prevent you from going wrong but you shouldn't need to rely on them to keep you right. In this section we provide a short list of common basic rules for trading Options that will hopefully help you through your initial trading executions and throughout your trading career:

- Contract pricing: In general Options trade in increments of $0.01, $0.05, and $0.10.
- Option premium: The price of the premium that you pay for an option is obtained by multiplying the option price offered by the multiplier. When trading in stocks the multiplier value is usually based upon 100 shares of the underlying stock. Therefore, when you purchase one option that is quoted at $2.80, you are actually going to have to pay $2,80 x 100 = $280 for the option, plus any broker commission.
- Market conditions: There are different market conditions that impact both the stock and options markets. These include the following:
- Trading halts for a security or entire market: If you find yourself holding an option for a halted stock, them the any options based on the stock will also be halted. This does not affect your rights or prevent you from exercising your contract rights. However be aware that when this occurs before expiration it may be difficult to trade the options but will not prevent you from exercising the option on or before the expiry date.
- Fast trading conditions: In fast-moving markets stock prices can change rapidly and you are likely to see quotes changing quickly. As a result when you are placing an order you might find that there are significant delays. This can simply be because your bid is not falling out with the bid-ask spread so is being ignored. Therefore you need to check and if necessary to edit your order to make it more acceptable. Also in fast moving market conditions make sure to use limit orders that are price focused rather

than market orders as you may end up paying more than you wanted.

- Booked order: In the case of a booked order – one that a market maker places that improve the current market quote. You may encounter problems filling these types of orders for Options greater than 1 contract and you are likely to only get a partial fill of the order. Be aware of this if using ALL or No parameters on your order.

- Best-execution: Execution quality is a measure of a broker's ability to fill orders at, or better than, the current market for the security. Options exchanges are required to monitor and send a daily exception report to your broker whenever a trade is executed at a price other than at the NBBO, referred to as traded-through. If you are unhappy with the price on transactions or are finding it hard to make a trade on what appears to be competitive prices you will need to contact your Broker for an explanation.

Finding a Broker and a Platform

Finding a suitable Brokerage account is a critical activity for any serious investor looking to trade Option in the market. Not all online brokers are suited to options trading however and some have very strict rules, which are serious constraints on a beginner's activities. Interestingly, as options are becoming more main-stream and are finally being seen as a way to manage risk and use leverage rather than a field for reckless speculation things are improving. Indeed many brokers are beginning to welcome beginners in options trading as they now view them as serious risk-aware traders that are diversifying into options to boost their profits.

However for the investor it is still a problem finding a suitable brokerage because it is true that any broker can buy and sell stocks, but not all of them have the skills, knowledge and the online tools to help their clients in establishing and executing options-based transactions and strategies. Nonetheless, each year more brokerages are stepping up to the plate with improved portfolios of services aimed at the options trader. So, here are some of the things that you'll want to be looking out for when you're searching for an options broker.

1. Tools to assess options strategies

Evaluating and selecting appropriate options involves different analysis and information than picking the underlying stocks. Picking options on that stock will require looking at measures of market conditions, bid-ask spread, implied volatility, probability, and open interest, and trading behavior in order to come up with successful strategies.

The best online options brokers will have the specialist tools and analysis charts to help you evaluate which options are a good match with your trading strategy. They will also be able to provide access to trading simulators, historical and current market data, analytical platforms, and easy to navigate quote and order functions.

2. A trading platform that works with your strategy

Trading options can be very complicated especially when you advance into using risk-defined combination strategies to manage and risk and limit losses. Most beginners will start out simply buying or selling single Call or Put options on a particular stock. However, as their skills and experience develop they will gravitate towards using more advanced options strategies, which requires building a trading strategy by buying or selling combinations of different types of options. Constructing and coordinating the deployment of these strategies is very difficult unless your options broker's trading platform support these types of strategies. Ideally, they should be available as a turn-key option and selectable from a menu whereby the platform will do all the heavy-lifting in constructing these multi-leg combination orders.

The best trading platforms will have simple interfaces that make it easy to navigate and are intuitive to use so that you know exactly what you're doing. To most traders the platform is the broker so if you are comfortable with the trading experience then you will be happy with your options broker.

3. Make sure your broker's customer service agents know options

Although the vast amount of transactions will go solely through the broker's online trading platform, there will inevitably come a time when something goes wrong. This is when customer support becomes important as you will probably need to talk directly to a customer service agent in order to resolve your issue. This is when it becomes imperative that you speak to an experienced agent who can help resolve your issue quickly and efficiently.

Unfortunately, for many brokerage firms, options are a new service that they are entering into, and regular customer service agents aren't well trained or are not experienced enough in options to communicate and resolve issues effectively. The problem is that you cannot really evaluate a brokerage firm's customer service until you need their help and by that time it could be too late. However if you go with a broker that specializes in options, they are more likely to have options specialists working in the customer service department that you can communicate with when you need them. It is also a very good sign if the brokerage has invested in omnichannel communication support and technology like bots and robot-advisors as that can greatly speed up the issue resolution process.

4. Check Commissions are Competitive

Commissions on options trading can be a thorny issue as they are often obscure and for a good reason as often they are a lot higher than standard stock commissions. So it's important not to assume that broker that has a good reputation for low-prices with stocks will be so generous with options. This is down to the economics as most options markets are a lot less liquid than the markets for individual stocks so there isn't the same economy of scale.

Sometimes, you'll have to work with standard stock commissions and then add on an additional commission for the option. Others thankfully will just charge a one-off fee for each option transaction (2-leg). However there are several other fees you need to be aware of with options, such as margin charges and exercise transaction fees so you will need to dig through the fine print as sometimes the fees to exercise an option can be excessive.

Nonetheless, it is certainly true, that often you get what you pay for and in some cases, paying higher commissions will be worth the price if it equates to high-quality service.

5. Get trained on options

It is actually in the broker's interest to educate you in options trading or any financial trading for that matter. As not only will you use those services you will likely be more competent and take up less of their time trying to resolve your mistakes. However, some brokers are better than others and go a lot further than is strictly required to educate their clients in strategies, tactics and transaction processes. Most brokers will have freely available educational materials mainly online videos about options trading and these are often comprehensive catalogues covering just about every technical aspect of the business. This is in the broker's interest as it provides promotional material as well as a form of lock-in as all the demos have been performed on their own platform. Hence it may be considered a red-flag if a broker has little in the way of educational material or free demos/accounts. However at the very minimum every brokerage is required to give you disclosure documents from the Options Clearing Commission.

Education, guidance and technical support on options trading can take place on many types of media. A good combination of online videos, webinars, online FAQ and accessible customer service specialists through voice, chat and email is probably a gold standard. But remember you get what you are willing to pay for – after all a brokerage is a business as well and they cannot be expected to provide a Rolls-Royce service yet charge rock-bottom commissions. If you are willing to accept the trade-off you can get you what you need to be a more effective options investor at the price you are willing to pay.

Spend time evaluating brokerages, try out their demo platforms if you can and be diligent in finding the best broker that matches your needs as getting it wrong could cost you serious money.

To trade options well, you will need to have a good options broker. Then you will make the most of the opportunities that arise and that trading in options gives you.

There are many online brokers that beginners can use for trading options and several of the top ones don't even require you to fund an account. This makes them very attractive for testing and practicing on when experimenting with order types and paper trading. The most notable is in no particular order:

- **Interactive Brokers** – Cheapest around with no per-leg base fee, lowest margin rates are and dozens of options-oriented lessons - Account Minimum: $0 Fees: $0.005 per share

-

- **TD Ameritrade** (think or swim)- High-quality educational tool, which has live content on TDAmeritradeNetwork.com, it also has a trading simulator for practicing options trading strategies, the platform also has many tools for selecting options strategies, as well as streaming data available on all platforms - Account Minimum: $0 Fees: $6.95 for stock and ETF trades, $6.95 per leg plus $0.75 for options

-

- **Charles Schwab** (StreetSmart platforms) – very good beginner Options-oriented trading lessons, with a wide array of asset classes that can be traded on any of the available platforms - Account Minimum: $0 Fees: $4.95 per stock and ETF trade, $0 for Schwab ETFs and $4.95 plus $0.65 per contract for options

-

- **Tastyworks** - Very stable platform, All the tools are accessible from a single page, The platform is focused on derivatives trading Account Minimum: $0 Fees: $5.00 stock trades $1.00 options trades

All of the online brokers suggested above have a variety of features and tools, some are better than others and some are a lot cheaper than others so it is something of a trade-off. The most important thing is to try some out and find one that matches your own budget and requirements.

Understanding Transaction Fees and Slippage

Broker fees across the trading world vary greatly as can be seen from the sample listed above. However saying that they do all tend to charge fees based upon per transactions or leg (2 legs per transaction a buy and a sell) and something that they call slippage.

Slippage is the term used to account for the difference between a quoted price and the actual price you pay or are paid for a stock. In today's fast markets slippage has become unavoidable as prices change so rapidly. The amount of price slippage is determined by the difference between the bid and the asking price - the spread. The larger the spread the more likely there will be significant slippage, as it's a sign of low liquidity and volume.

There are two ways to approach minimizing slippage:

1. Use limit orders instead of market orders – Limit orders will only execute at the price you set, market orders on the other hand will always fill the order at the best available price and that is the primary cause of slippage.
2. Consider slippage to be a cost of doing business – If using limit orders is unsuitable – in many cases they are as there will be times that you must guarantee opening or closing a position – then you must calculate the likely cost of slippage into the financials.

Options Trading Simplified

The ways to calculate slippage - as a cost of doing business, just like all the other fees and commissions - is to use the following formula:

Amount of bid-ask spread in dollars x 100 (shares) x 1 (contract) x 2 (legs (open/close)) = slippage

Develop a Small Account Trading Strategy

Beginners always want to know how much money they need in their fund to be able to trade successfully. The truth of the matter is that you can trade happily with a small fund of 5,000 dollars it is just with a small account you have to be very sensitive to risk. That means making small percentage trades on high probability, high volatility options and always ensuring that your positions are risk defined and covered. Therefore a simple trading strategy for a small beginner account would be to adhere to the following pointers:

- Trade using small allocations for each trade
- Trade using risk defined strategies (always covered and never naked)
- Trade those high probability Options (pick the low hanging fruit)
- Trade in high Implied Volatility (IV) Options
- Build long term consistency – use the big numbers

When you first start out trading it is imperative that you protect your capital fund and that means only making a small allocation for each trade. A general rule of thumb on an account of around $5,000 would be to limit your allocation to 1%-2% per trade. You can later when you become more experienced start to look to 2%-3% allocation but you should never need to go higher. It is always better to make several small allocations per trade than being over-committed on a single trade.

Another reason for having a small account trading strategy is that trading at the end of the day is driven by probability and percentages (returns on investment) rather than purely on dollar returns. There is no reason at all why you cannot trade on a $5,000 account if you remember that it's more about managing the risk rather than the dollar stakes. For example, with a $5000 fund and you take allocations of 1% ($50) per trade and you have a run of trades that go against you that will be bad but not catastrophic. However if you start out taking 5% allocation ($250) or worse 10% ($500) allocations things go wrong exponentially quicker and leave you cleaned out in no time.

Placing too large allocations per trade is a path to ruin so bear in mind to keep it low. This may be frustrating at first as there will be some attractive trades that you will want to make but simply you cannot risk. In these cases you must be disciplined and not make the trade - never trade over your allocation or your account size as that is the surest way to get cleaned out.

After all as you can build up your fund using small allocations on high probability trades over time and then you can start to allocate more dollars but the percentages should stay the same regardless of the equity fund size.

The second point in our strategy is to always have a risk defined position as with small accounts we do need to guard against excessive or unlimited risk. Therefore we want to be using well-defined trading strategies which limit our risk exposure. The one thing you must never do is go naked as that is inviting unlimited risk and to be cleaned out should the trade go against you. There are many safe risk defined strategies that we can use even with small accounts to make small profits. And the thing is if we concentrate our efforts on high probability trades and making more consistent and frequent trades whereby we are winning more often than we lose. This is why sticking to consistently making small frequent high probability trades is so important for small accounts.

Gradually that account will soon start to build up as we will have the law of big numbers and the percentages firmly on our side, which makes things a lot more predictable and profitable.

Deploying Risk-Defined Techniques

In the strategy that we have just looked at for Options trading with a small fund there was a recommendation to use risk-defined trades. In this section we will look at how we make these risk defined or risk-capped trades such as Credit Spreads, Iron Condors and Butterfly Spreads.

Now the first thing that often springs to mind is that in Options trading we are working with limited risk trades anyway as if setup correctly we should only we at risk of losing our premium. But the beauty of combining Calls and Puts in sophisticated ways means that we can construct some really elegant risk-defined strategies. A good example is in the classic credit spread strategy.

Credit Spread Strategy

A Credit Spread is a risk-defined strategy that involves combining two Call orders. The way it works is that you will need to buy a call with one strike price, and then sell (write) a call with a lower strike price.

Now, if we look at the differences between the call Options, one was bought with a strike price of let's say $39 for $0.15. But if you then write a call Option with a strike price of $32 for $1.27. You now have a net credit position of $1.27 − $0.15 = $1.12. Now, your overall position is out-of-the-money but that means it is profitable to you the writer and will remain so as long as the underlying price is below $32.

Should the price reach $32 dollar the option may well be exercised. That would mean getting assigned the option and you would have to buy the underlying asset at market value. In this case your loss would be the market price less $32. However, if the underlying price were at $39 or above, you could exercise your long call to limit your loss. Hence, your maximum loss would be $39.00 − $32.00 − $1.12 = $5.88.

However, with the technique of combining different types of orders we can construct sophisticated trading strategies that tightly define-risk or even cap risk. For example let's look at the Iron Condor, which is a great beginner strategy because it is both non-directional and also range bound.

Iron Condor

An Iron Condor is a suitable beginner strategy for selling a range-bound stock position for a steady income. The way it works is that it requires you to make several Calls and Puts that define the upper and lower ranger boundaries. So for example we need to:

- Sell a Put and then Buy a Put at a lower strike price – basically create a Put spread
- Sell a Call and then Buy a Call at a higher strike price – basically create a Call spread

The logic behind the Iron Condor is that the strategy creates range-boundaries between the two sold points. So long as the traffic, which can move in any direction, stays within the range-boundaries, the strategy will earn money – premiums.

The Iron Condor strategy will only lose money should the trade move out with the bounded range formed by the two spreads.

Covered Calls

These are another good beginner strategy as they can provide profit when a stock is flat, moving sideways or falling just slightly. To be covered is essential in the risk-defined strategy so you need to buy 100 shares in stock then sell a Call option for the 100 shares. The trade will then make money so long as the stock goes up, remains flat or even if it dips slightly.

The way this works is that the money collected through the premiums not only provided some protection against a fall in price but also enhances the returns when the stock stays flat.

Married Put Strategy

This is a rather sophisticated strategy that is suited to beginners due to its risk definition. The married Put works because like in the covered stock you have to combine an Option with a physical stock. In this case you would buy 100 shares in a stock. Then the key is to buy long put options for the equivalent number of shares. As a result the married put strategy works like an insurance policy against short-term losses. Then you need to buy long call options with a specific strike price. At the same time, you'll sell the same number of call options at a higher strike price. This makes the Married Put profits tied to the underlying stocks price performance, as you will need it to rise to make a profit but the added benefit is any downside is completely covered.

Protective Collar Strategy

This is another risk-defined trading strategy that like the covered spread is based upon the trader holding shares of the underlying stock. The trader can then buy protective puts and then sell call options against the stock holding. The puts and the calls are both chosen to be out-of-the-money options but they must have the same expiration date. Another caveat is that the stock must be equal in number to the options. For example 100 shares against 1 contract OTM Put, 1 contract OTM Call.

The way that it works will be that the investor will buy an out-of-the-money put option and simultaneously write an out-of-the-money call option for the same stock. The protected collar is a good strategy to use to protect the price of the underlying security whilst also providing a source of income via premium for the covered calls.

Long Straddle Strategy

With the long straddle strategy the trader will buy a call option and a put option at the same time. The way that it works is that both options must have the same strike price and the same expiration date. The strike price is at-the-money or as close to it as possible. The strategy is to make a profit from a significant shift in the price of the underlying stock regardless of the direction. The long straddle strategy is deployed when it is expected that a stock will move from a low volatility state to a much higher one and it is geared to benefit if the price moves in either direction. Typically a trader will set up along straddle just before an important news event is about to break to capture the sudden burst in trading volatility. The long straddle strategy has limited risk and unlimited potential for profit.

Long Strangle Strategy

Another form of unlimited profit but limited risk strategy is to use the long strangle strategy. In this case the investor will buy an out-of-the-money call option and an out of money put option at the same time. The two options will need to have the same expiration date but they will have different strike prices. The put strike price should always be lower than the call strike price. Large gains can be made using the long strangle if there is sufficient change in volatility before the expiry date but it is a debit spread at setup.

Putting it all together

Throughout this book, we have strived to teach you how to start successfully trading options. In the course of your studies you have learned much of the theory and concepts behind options as financial instruments and how they are traded. You have also learned how to read an options table and an options chain to find those elusive options that meet your trading ambitions. You now know how to open and close positions using a number of orders that are suited to specific trading conditions and markets. Finally, and very importantly you have learned how to run your trading operations as a business and to trade like a professional. Crucially, you will have learned and understood the importance of having a trading strategy. To this purpose we proposed an advanced trading strategy that is suitable for beginners. The five-point strategy is designed to provide tracing longevity and make profits even in the most difficult markets. However, it is not a pick and mix list, you must adhere to all five principles to be successful. This is because it is not a bundle of trading tactics, it's a mindset, a philosophy, which if you develop it early in your trading career and stick with it, then you will greatly increase your chances of surviving long term. Successful traders are measured by their longevity and not their short term gains as luck can distort that picture immensely. And luck doesn't last forever but a good strategy, which enforces best practices and risk management does make you a better trader.

After reading this book you now have all the knowledge necessary to trade in options and a sound strategy on which to base your trading career. But this should be only the start of your education as in options trading – every day's a school day. It has taken you 7 days or less to learn how to make money trading options – now it's time to step up and start trading.

Good Luck and Healthy Profits!

Thank you

Before you go, I just wanted to say thank you for purchasing my book.

You could have picked from dozens of other books on the same topic but you took a chance and chose this one.

So, a HUGE thanks to you for getting this book and for reading all the way to the end.

Now I wanted to ask you for a small favor. **Could you please consider posting a review on the platform? Reviews are one of the easiest ways to support the work of authors.**

This feedback will help me continue to write the type of books that will help you get the results you want. So if you enjoyed it, please let me know.

www.ingramcontent.com/pod-product-compliance
Lightning Source LLC
Chambersburg PA
CBHW060932220326
41597CB00020BA/3722